NEGRO and JEW

An Encounter in America

NEGRO
and
JEW

An Encounter in America

A Symposium Compiled by *Midstream* Magazine

Shlomo Katz, *Editor*

The Macmillan Company, New York

Collier-Macmillan Limited, London

The articles in this book are reprinted from the December
1966 issue of *Midstream* magazine, Copyright © 1966 by
The Theodor Herzl Foundation, Inc., and reprinted by
permission of the contributors and of the Publisher.

Library of Congress Catalog Card Number: 67-23622

First Printing
The Macmillan Company, New York
Collier-Macmillan Canada Ltd., Toronto, Ontario
PRINTED IN THE UNITED STATES OF AMERICA

CONTENTS

PREFACE

IT IS now widely accepted as an incontrovertible fact that, 1) there exists a pronounced anti-Jewish sentiment among the Negro masses in this country, despite the active participation of many idealistic young Jews in the Negro struggle for equal rights, and the moral support given to the Civil Rights Movement by organized Jewish groups, and, 2) that Jews are reacting to this sentiment with an emotional backlash. Though no exact studies of substantial reliable data about this situation are available, the prevalence of anti-Jewish myths among Negroes is undeniable. Thus, "Mr. Goldberg" has come to be regarded by many Negroes as a symbol of their oppression, second only to "Mr. Charlie." The "Jewish slumlord" has become in Negro ghettos a synonym for the exploiting owner of cheap sub-standard housing, as if Jews were a major factor in the ownership and management of real estate in the ghettos. Jewish-owned enterprises in the Negro ghettos are often regarded by Negroes as the epitome of their economic exploitation, in disregard of the fact that, at most, these account for a minute share of Negro economic misery, which is primarily caused by large industrial or agricultural enterprises in which the Negro is excluded from employment or exploited at its lowest levels. In the rioting that erupted in Harlem, Watts and other Negro centers during the past couple of years, a large proportion of the businesses destroyed were Jewish owned.

Many Jews, on their part, react with special resentment to anti-Semitic sentiments among Negroes. They point out that Jews have not been historically partners to the Negro enslavement and oppression in the United States. They feel particularly bitter because Jews have been the victims of the greatest racist crime in human history, perpetrated in our own time by white nations, and they regard it as adding insult to grave injury when they are not only lumped by Negroes together with "whitey" but are also singled out for special hostility.

Many Jews become defensive and tend to blame Negroes for part of their woes. After outbreaks such as the one in Watts, they tend to withdraw financial and other support they have previously given to the cause of Negro freedom, and to call for self-isolation within the Jewish community.

Leaders among Negroes have tended to underestimate the importance of the manifestation of anti-Jewishness among Negroes, claiming that it is in fact an expression of special identification with Jews: Negroes expect more from Jews, these leaders maintain, precisely because Jews have suffered oppression and are therefore expected to show more understanding of the Negro situation and greater empathy with them; when Negroes do not find this, they react with special resentment.

Among Jews, on the other hand, this hostility on the part of a fellow-ethnic minority arouses historical memories of parallel situations in their former domiciles, where other oppressed groups vented their misery on the easiest target at hand—the small Jewish minority.

This condition of growing misunderstanding between Jews and Negroes in America has reached the point where candid discussion is urgently needed if it is to be halted and reversed. Lacking exact and detailed data, it is only possible to turn to informed opinion based on experience with the relations of the two groups. It is the aim of this symposium to provide a broad cross-section of such opinion. The questions proposed cannot, in the nature of things, comprehend the entire complex of factors that determine Negro-Jewish relations and attitudes, nor are direct answers to them always possible. It is rather their purpose to serve as broad guidelines for the examination of an evolving social development which, if not faced and clarified, may in time become ominous.

1. Do you regard anti-Semitic sentiments among Negroes as an earnest menace to Jewish well-being as well as to the interests of the Negro population by diverting its attention from the true interests of the movement for Negro civil rights and equality?

2. How do you assess the prevalence and weight of the Jewish backlash to Negro anti-Semitism?

3. Was there, in your estimation, a pronounced anti-Jewish

aspect to the destruction in the course of the rioting in Negro ghettos during the past two years?

4. Are Jews disproportionately represented in the ownership of low-cost housing and in retail distribution in the ghettos?

5. If the answer to the preceding question is affirmative, should special efforts be made by Jewish communal leaders, both lay and spiritual, to dissuade Jews from setting up businesses in the Negro ghettos where, in times of disturbance, they are likely to find themselves in the first line of fire?

6. Do Jews seek to identify themselves culturally and socially with white American society to the point of losing the realization that, historically, they have been victims of white Christian civilization even more than have the Negroes in America?

7. Do Jews, because of the ethics of their religion, and because of their historical experience as a persecuted group, owe a special debt of greater participation in the Negro liberation movement than their Christian neighbors?

8. Have the rabbinate, in all its ramifications, and the lay Jewish organizations, contributed their proper share to the Negro liberation movement?

9. Has the Negro leadership done its full duty to counteract anti-Jewish sentiments among the Negro masses?

10. To what extent do the Muslim cults, popular among the Negro population, exacerbate the hostility to Jews by projecting onto the American scene a distorted image of Arab hostility to Israel?

11. Would it prove helpful to establish special Negro-Jewish consultative bodies to examine misunderstandings between the two groups as these arise, and to foster greater understanding between them on the basis of common historical experiences of oppression, dispersion and minority status?

INTRODUCTION

THE VOICE on the phone trembled with indignation. "Where do you live? I bet you live in a safe white neighborhood and have your office in a safe area in mid-Manhattan. Do you know what it means to fear attack every time you walk down the street? If you did, you wouldn't talk that way. . . . You're just another Jewish self-hater. . . . You don't care what happens to your own people. . . ." and the voice trailed off into incoherent hysteria.

This phone call was but the first after I had published a letter in a liberal Jewish periodical shortly after some Negro rioting during which numerous Jewish stores were sacked. The letter protested an editorial that, it seemed to me, was hectoring, and that smugly boasted how "we," Jews, that is, had all along stood "in the front ranks" of the struggle for Negro rights, and vaguely threatened that unless "responsible" Negro leadership ("if there are responsible Negro leaders") puts a stop to outbreaks of violence "we," while remaining liberal, might nevertheless be driven to some sort of agonizing reappraisal.

For nearly a week after the first call my line was busy. The anonymous callers would always begin with a reasonable appeal for understanding the plight of Jews living or conducting their businesses within or on the margins of Negro ghettos, their sense of insecurity, the violence they were subject to. Then would follow bitterly sarcastic requests for advice as to what they should do under the circumstances, and finally a deluge of vituperation, sometimes accompanied by threats. On a few occasions the callers would put their argument on a personal level: "What's the matter? Aren't you scared of Negro hoodlums and muggers?" But all attempts to answer this question with statements that I was indeed very much afraid of muggers and hoodlums, but not especially so because they were black; that I was probably more afraid of

white anti-Jewish violence; and that any Jew of our generation, remembering what the white Germans, in cooperation
with other European whites, did to us within our own
memory, could not, must not, allow himself to fall into the
trap of associating anti-Semitism and its concomitant violence with Negroes in particular were wasted effort, for
the voices on the phone were genuinely urgent with fear
and confusion and anger, and, above all, with surprise.
Beneath the furious taunts of "nigger lover," "self-hater,"
"traitor," could be discerned the bewilderment of people
caught unawares. How could this happen in America? How
could this happen to us who are relatively recent newcomers
to the American scene and are not part of the Negro-
white tragedy that has been in the making for three centuries?

In the course of our long history, and especially during
the past nineteen centuries of dispersion, we Jews have
come in contact, for better or for worse, with many peoples.
We have been in Spain and in Poland, in Germany and in
Russia, in France and in Rumania. But it was not until we
came to America in substantial numbers that we encoun-
tered the black race. In the dim beginnings of our history
the problem of Negro-Jewish relations had briefly cropped
up in the somewhat ominous and vaguely outlined story
of Moses and the Cushite wife he had taken, how his
brother and sister, Aaron and Miriam, resented this alliance, and how they were punished for it. But this encounter, wrapped in the fog of mythology, had no followup.
Here and there a Negro appears peripherally in ancient
Jewish history, in the entourage of King David, for instance,
but this contact is ephemeral. Our encounters, our loves
and hates, unfolded their destinies in the European and
Mediterranean world.

And then we came en masse to America. We learned
English, we traversed the odyssey from sweatshop to a measure of affluence, we became active in the economic, political, and academic life of the country, but for more than a
generation we remained virtually oblivious of the millions of
Negroes as an important part of the American scene.

In the course of our struggle of adaptation, it seems we have made some grave errors. Granted that New York's Jewish ghetto on the Lower East Side was remote from the Negro concentrations in the South. Still, in terms of our history in the United States, this obliviousness to the Negro presence in the country and to its implications for the future is not entirely forgivable. For the Jewish masses who streamed to this country at the turn of the century were not a shapeless mob rushing blindly from persecution to a haven of safety. These were people with an ancient history and long experience in the implications of living among both majorities and other minorities in eastern Europe. And these Jewish immigrant masses had an informed, sophisticated, and articulate leadership—the same leadership that by means of communal organization and economic struggle led them within a brief period from ghetto slums to an enviable status of welfare and equality. But these same leaders who organized the big strikes in the garment industries early in the century, who set up huge fraternal organizations for education and mutual assistance, who were informed about and responsive to the needs of oppressed people a continent away remained strangely unaware of the problems of the Negroes living in the same country with them.

Another error consisted in the failure to see America in all its complexity, culturally, historically, and ethnically. At first glance the immigrant, and only too often, his leaders, saw America as a kind of deracinated social and political entity that operated mechanically on the basis of a set of noble principles enunciated in the Constitution, that, except for some ignoble and temporary exceptions that presumably only proved the rule, opportunity was really unrestricted, and, given suitable effort and an appropriate IQ, all obstacles could be overcome. For a time, this faulty vision seemed to operate. Hence much of the surprise when it broke down and when we are now made painfully aware that America is not simply a geographical aggregate of so many millions of individual citizens entitled to equal rights, which, with some effort, can be implemented in practice.

This may very well account for the confusion now surrounding the concept of integration, for instance. Seized upon as the natural banner in the struggle for Negro rights, it has quickly become problematic. In a deracinated society of millions of political entities, it might be ideal. But what if we are not merely citizens of the United States? What if we are at the same time Jews, Negroes, Mexicans, Puerto Ricans? What if some, perhaps a growing number, of the Negroes do not wish to integrate to the point of ethnic or cultural disintegration? For though the prophetic ideal of the ultimate unity of the race of man is no doubt the highest that the human mind has conceived, it cannot be expected to serve as a practical solution for problems that are contemporary and that demand other solutions.

Nor have Jews who think along Zionist lines been more sensitive to the emerging pattern of Negro evolution in this country. This is distressing because of the numerous similarities between the two groups. Not only do both share a status of minority and dispersion, but the evolution of their groups and national consciousness has in many respects followed along parallel lines. Yet when the slogan of Black Power was raised recently, with its primary aim of placing the Negro struggle for equality in Negro hands, even avowed Zionists failed to perceive that such too were the beginnings of the Jewish national liberation movement in Europe, commencing with Pinsker's *Autoemancipation* down through *kibbush avodah* and the other stages of Zionist evolution, and that these aims, like the Black Power movement, required that somewhere along the line something would have to give, someone would have to move to make room for the new aspirants with a just claim not only to equality but to their own identity.

Not last to feel discomfited by the new demands of the Negro movement were those idealistic and self-sacrificing young Jews who had abandoned the comforts that were theirs for the asking and joined the Negro struggle at its very cutting edge. Imbued with the noblest sentiments, they are now told that they are no longer wanted, not too closely anyway. And they are dismayed.

As a by-product of our recent Jewish history, and growing out of its frustrations, we have given rise to small but articulate and competent cadres of idealistic youth, who with a full knowledge of the geography of revolution and social regeneration are ever-ready to lend their talents wherever these occur. It is not pleasant, and now comes as a shock, to be told by Negro fellow-militants, "We don't need you any longer. We don't want you in our midst. We prefer to do our self-liberating ourselves, even if we don't do it as well or as fast as you." (In much the same way, Chairman Nikita Khrushchev not so many years ago told the leaders of the Polish Communist Party, "There are too many Rabinoviches among you.")

Even on the level of emotional perception, there has arisen a tragic distance of misapprehension. Nobody in his right senses will justify the violence, and some of the slogans under which it has recently been conducted, in Negro ghettos. But the depth of the anger behind it should have been understood. Yet the same people who read as Holy Scripture outbursts of anger over an ancient wrong, such as, "Pour out thy wrath upon the nations . . . for they have devoured Jacob and laid waste his dwelling place" (Psalms, 79), or, "O daughter of Babylon . . . happy shall be he that taketh and dasheth thy little ones against the stones" (Psalms, 138), fail to understand the rage next door.

Is this because we, as Jews, have lost the capacity for great anger? Is it that, because we suffer from a measure of confusion about the meaning of our own identity and recent history, the necessary element of empathy is missing?

And on the Negro side there is the temptation to isolate Jews as the target of their anger for inexcusable, even if facile, reasons. For one thing, Jews are an easy, and historically speaking, a socially acceptable target. They are also a safe and readily accessible one. That in the long run this choice is likely to be morally degrading, no less than slavery was for the white slave owners, does not alter the situation, and must be reckoned with in assessing the future relations between the two groups and what steps should be taken to avoid tragedy.

Negroes and Jews—two dispersed minorities, both harboring deep grievances against their treatment by the white

Christian world—now meet in America. The Jews are over-whelmingly urban; Negroes are rapidly becoming so. They live next to each other; indeed, one follows in the footsteps of the other in the geography of the cities. They have never met in the past. There are no ancient wrongs between them to poison their attitudes toward one another. Here is one instance in which two groups can begin their mutual relations with a clean slate. Yet the horizon between them is becoming clouded with misunderstandings and resentments. A thorough examination of the situation has become an urgent necessity, and it is the purpose of this symposium to contribute to that purpose.

SHLOMO KATZ

NEGRO and JEW

An Encounter in America

JOEL CARMICHAEL

THE MOST curious element in the current discussion among Jews of the "Negro problem" seems to me to be its emphasis on duty.

Jews and Negroes are both being "called upon," it seems, to handle each other with kid gloves because of a similar record of suffering.

This, while wholly understandable, I think lays too great a burden on ordinary people.

Jews *should* not, of course, be prejudiced against Negroes, who in their turn *should* not dislike Jews.

Yet what could be more natural than for many Negroes, gripped by a general prejudice against white people (though I think this fantastically exaggerated, especially by some Negro "spokesmen"), to pick out the weakest sector of the white population, knowing that the Jews are both vulnerable and feeble and, perhaps more importantly, are themselves disliked by other whites? Negroes who have such feelings can have their cake and eat it: they can dislike white people and simultaneously be copying them. The existence of this phenomenon among Russian peasants under tsarism merely shows how "natural" it is.

But though Jews do not, to my mind, *owe* Negroes anything special beyond the extension to them of the fairness that Jews *should* extend to everyone, I don't think that Jews—simply as a fact—have any anti-Negro prejudice to speak of in comparison with White America. I think ordinary Jews *do*, by and large, feel sympathy for ordinary Negroes; the "backlash" among Jews seems to me insignificant. If anything, I think Jews, especially Jewish liberals—a word that on this question at least surely takes in a very large proportion of Jews—are far too indulgent with respect to those Negro intellectuals who have made a sort of career out of kicking liberals in the teeth, especially Jewish liberals. Such Jews set themselves absurdly high standards, as though they were being called upon to ameliorate the plight of the Negroes all by themselves. They listen far too sheepishly to many self-appointed Negro speakers and writers who have utilized a combination of neurosis and cynicism to carve out a minor eminence as public figures.

The fact that Negroes have no real complaints about Jews as such does not mean that a mythical (i.e., prejudiced) attitude toward the Jews is not natural to them. It doesn't matter at all whether there are *really* more Jewish landlords, grocers, etc., than there "should" be; nor is it possible to shunt Jewish landlords away from areas where they may see a landlord's opportunity, or to diminish the total number of Jews in the real-estate business. Jewish landlords and grocers are no worse than others, but that won't help them if Negroes vent a perfectly natural spleen on the Jews for sociopsychological reasons of their own that Jews cannot in the nature of things control. Landlords too, after all, *should* not be *too* rapacious. Much good saying *that* does!

Contrariwise, the disproportionate number of Jewish boys and girls in the various branches of the Civil Rights Movement is also not going to be chalked up to the credit of Jews as such by any Negroes in the clutch of anti-Semitism; such Negroes will not strike a balance between greedy Jewish grocers and idealistic Jewish marchers.

To my mind, accordingly, it is silly to ask ordinary Jews or Jewish leaders to tie themselves in knots either to placate anti-Semitic Negroes or to do something beyond their power—"to contribute their proper share to the Negro liberation movement." They are already contributing far more than their "proper" share; I find this both commendable and historically appropriate. To demand of Jews more than they are doing at present seems to me a form of Jewish self-flagellation than can help no one.

As for the Negro leadership, why should they "counteract" anti-Semitism insofar as it exists among the Negro masses? They may be anti-Semites themselves, after all, though of course they *should* not be.

Historically, I should think, Jews and Negroes represent

antithetical social ailments. The Jews are alienated at least partly by an excess of individuation as a collectivity; their Scriptures alone have given them so much self-awareness and also, surely, so much morale that their identity as a people, despite the abundance of neurotic attitudes in individuals, is of rocklike firmness. Negroes, on the contrary, have as a people no singularity of historical background to refer to. They have been hampered in their formation of a collective identity by two things: their mutilated, excluded situation in White America, and the atomized, tribal multiplicity of their universes in Africa, though I need hardly say that the "ethnic" connection between Negro America and Negro Africa is a mere fantasy.

In both Africa and America, after all, the very concept of a "Negro race" merely reflects the racist attitudes of white people lumping everything together. It is no more than an irony of history that Negro intellectuals have been trapped into the acceptance of these curiously vulgar clichés—"Negro race," "Negro people"—precisely by their disadvantaged position in both continents. In America even the biological element is remarkably exiguous: despite the extraordinary variety of skin colorations, physical types, etc., in the communities classed by racist Americans as "Negro," the Negro community as a whole is treated in a special category. This is simply a caste situation; its rigidity has nothing to do with biology and still less with culture, since the Negroes are in all respects simply Americans—Americans suffering from an American disease.

In Africa the only thing relevant to the lives of most Africans has been, historically, the great cozy, tribal universes, which do not regard themselves as "Negro" at all— an idea that is quite simply meaningless—but as members of one tribe or another. Of course this situation has been changing rapidly in the past few generations, but even so the change has not penetrated very far and in any case the pulverization of tribal life has not been succeeded by the formation of a new axis of collective identity, least of all in the newly emergent "states." These are mere ramshackle bureaucratic hangovers of the colonial period that have landed in the laps of various coteries, some of them adven-

turers, some idealists, all divided from each other by the
scramble for power within generally small, impoverished
and historically incoherent administrative contrivances.

What is absolutely senseless in connection with both Negro
Americans and Black Africans is the very notion of "negritude"—as though there were anything in common between,
say, a Masai and an Ibo, except, very precisely, in the
mind of a white man indifferent to the real people behind
the many tribal names and lumping them all together, quite
irresponsibly, as "Negroes!"

It is obviously foolish to talk about a "Negro people" in
the sense one might about the "French people." There may
be—from a technical, taxonomic point of view—a "Negro
race," but there is no more a Negro people than there is a
white people. In Africa there is, of course, a Masai people,
a Zulu people etc.; but the idea of an African people is
obviously a white idea, and in view of the plain fact that
the great African tribal groups have neither a sense of
solidarity nor written monuments of their past, it is a mere
literary abstraction.

The fact that some Black African intellectuals, abetted
often by American Negroes and sometimes, of course, by
muddier-minded anthropologists, have accepted this non-
sensical rubric of "negritude" is itself a depressing symptom
of its insubstantiality.

In America the formation of Negro identity is crippled
by the inability of American Negroes to point to any cultural roots outside America. They are wholly American;
the occasional quest of individuals for roots in Africa is
simply pathetic, especially since the only prop of such a
quest can never be more than anthropological erudition,
provided, very often, by Jewish anthropologists!

I have mentioned Africa in connection with American
Negroes only because its existence is an additional disturbing factor in America; its very artificiality illustrates the
difference between the Jewish and the American Negro
"problems."

I think the Black Muslim movement in America is a
splendid illustration of this.

Islam, of course, exists; perhaps some ordinary American

Negroes have heard of it (I mean unlike most ordinary Americans). The so-called Muslim movement, however, has nothing to do with historic Islam, which embraces, after all, some five hundred million people, a lot of them white, vast numbers brown (Indonesians, etc.) and black, and a substantial number of bona fide Black Africans. This whole question of Islam is so much Greek to the American Negroes who have become Black Muslims.

These Black Muslims are a wholly American reaction to American life. The Muslim tag is simply a device for leaping over the ghetto walls in America—intellectually! —and claiming something outside America to act as a counterweight to the feeling of inferiority American Negroes suffer from simply as Americans. It is just because American Negroes can claim no culture uniquely their own that they lay claim to an enormous culture they have only dimly heard of, and heard only one aspect of: Islamic egalitarianism, which, because of their parochial situation in America, they have interpreted, quite absurdly, as meaning black *superiority!*

One of the most impressive things about the late Malcolm X was his ability to change his mind in the face of a fact; this is very unusual. Before going to Mecca he was categorically anti-white, in the style that has become modish; in Mecca he saw, to his stupefaction, that most Muslims were both non-Negro and non-racist. This simple perception would have enabled him to become, perhaps, a real Muslim, if he had had any religious goals and had been operating outside Negro America.

I don't think the Muslim movement among American Negroes stimulates anti-Semitism, though of course it may be true that confused American Negroes think their indigenous anti-Semitism is supported by something in the outside world. But it would be quite preposterous for any American Black Muslim to look for anti-Semitism in Islam; there is quite enough in America!

I suppose there may be some danger for Jews in Negro hostility; but the real danger is surely the savagery of white Americans, which seems to me an extraordinary phenomenon. Despite spasmodic and fundamentally, in some sense or other, justifiable outbursts in the Negro communities, Negroes by and large are absolutely angelic, if one thinks of what they are up against. I find it strange that the Negroes are as mild-mannered, sensible, and moderate as they are. Imagine confronting, day by day, the faces of southern lower-middle-class whites, contorted by vindictive cruelty! Imagine watching the ferocious northern whites in the slums of the big cities! People, including ordinary women, who can chant: "Burn, blackie, burn! Kill the jungle bunnies!" at the mere prospect of integration among school-children.

For Jew and Negro alike the enemy—perhaps the sole point of convergence—remains the unaccountable ferocity of such a large segment of American society.

The danger for the Jews is, perhaps, that they may be caught, individually or communally, between the two fires —for them an historical banality!—too white for Negro activists, too pro-Negro for white racists.

The danger for the Negroes remains acute for the simple reason that they are, after all, a very small minority, a minority that is, moreover, very hard to organize, educate and ideologize, and a substantial segment of which is out of touch with any self-conscious social influence. It has been estimated that perhaps a third of the American Negroes have simply opted out of society; they are just apathetic with respect to every social force; White America has made them too cynical for contact.

Thus Negroes will doubtless remain for a time the principal target for the vast amount of brutality lurking in the United States, and by virtue of this alone, perhaps, will go on acting as a shield for the Jews.

ARTHUR A. COHEN

SURELY ONE of the defects of the Jewish personality is that it collects itself (like a derelict rummaging in a junkyard for usable bits and pieces) from its environment, picking and gnawing at the social structures of others for reliable self-images, sources of confirmation and approval. It is a neurotic posture, but it should alarm no one that the Jewish personality, however assimilated (or, more fashionably, acculturated), is still resolutely neurotic. The neurosis—however variously it may be described—is transmitted from generation to generation and disappears only when the historical experience with which it must cope ceases to be either enthusiastically Jewish or explicitly anti-Jewish.

Jews, no less than other human animals, adapt more healthily to an environment which neither makes demands of conscience nor saps by derision the energy of its ego. The three hundred years of "the American experience" have not yet succeeded in alleviating the Jewish neurasthenia. We are as nervous, peevish, delicate and precarious as we have ever been. This somehow delights me. Although the pain obtrudes in nightmares and the sense of alienage comes like a sirocco, blowing from the wastes of the desert, unforewarned and desiccating, it is a helpful reminder that all is not well with my world, that I am unwell within it, that there is much to be done before I die.

My concern for the issue at hand, the explicit and articulate anti-Semitism of many Negroes, the anti-Semitism of radical Negro leadership, the anti-Semitism of some (I know and cannot name them) white Christians (and they are profoundly "Christocentric" Christians) masochists of the Negro revolt does not surprise nor alarm me. Not that I am unaware of the dangers of anti-Semitism or that I need reminder of the vengeful and murderous potentiality of anti-Semitism. Not at all. My lack of alarm and surprise results more from my sense of myself as a Jew (and my insistence upon the unnatural and ahistorical sources of the ultimate Jewish identity) than it does from any of the breast-beating of radical Jewish intelligentsia who regard Negro anti-Semitism as justified precisely because they have disengaged themselves from the values of American-Jewish mediocrity. They use the hatred of Negroes to beat their parents and flagellate their own psyches; I use the anti-Semitism of Negroes to confirm what I have always believed: what God wishes from the Jews and what world history uses them to justify are still incommensurable.

The anti-Semitism of the Negro—founded upon repetitious charges of economic and political exploitation—has of course more real justification than the same charges levelled by the economically impoverished peasant who depredated the Jews of the Rhineland in the time of the Crusades. In those days the Jew was a vulnerable substitute for the Church and the Lord. The peasant could transfer an unarticulated hatred from the real oppressor to the symbolic oppressor, from the real tyrant to the "Christkiller" through whose miscreancy a fallen world was permitted to remain fallen (and incidentally impoverished). But today no one denies that there are unnumerable small Jewish merchants in the Negro communities of the North who probably, like small merchants everywhere, are nagging, tough, charge excessive interest and carriage fees, etc. But these small Jewish merchants don't run the slums nor, by and large, do they own them. For instance, in the 'forties when I went to a large university in the mid-West, much of the Negro slum was owned directly or indirectly by the university, but cleverly (diabolically?) the rent collectors were by and large Jews. The Jews received the contempt and violence; the university received the rent. Court Jews of a different era, rent collectors, financing exploitation for a white and Christian community. The Jew is no more nor less than he has ever been, the viator and conduit of the hatred of one section of Christendom against another. The hatred of the Jew is the one psychic link, however, which exists between black and white Christians, the one unexpungeable, irrational, mythic connection which need not be abandoned, even though the white and Christian "devil" is the origin of oppression for both the black and the Jew.

It is interesting to note that the anti-Christianity of some sectors of the Negro community has no theological character —it is a rejection of the enforced passivity, self-abnegation, "know your place" in the universe, social ethic of Christian conversatism. The Negro reviles the Calvinist theology of anti-black Biblicism, for the Calvinism has supplied generations of white racists with divine authentication for hatred.

The existence of Negro anti-Semitism is indubitable. What is curious is the reaction of American Jews to it: indignation, anger, but even more an almost innocent sense of betrayal. At the base of this sense of betrayal may well be something more unsettling. For all his contentment in this new Zion, the Jew is never far from his anguish and his grief. I have never observed Jews in the urban North (I scarcely know the South) regard their position of economic power and influence as one threatened by the Civil Rights Movement. Quite the contrary, the Jewish community—out of all proportion to its size—has supported for more than a generation the cause of civil rights. Jewish support of civil rights cannot be put down as an activity of cleaning conscience or the expunction of guilt. It is an absolute and hardly formal expression of Jewish disdain for Christian hypocrisy, but not more than that. The Jews have been pretty damn good on civil rights. Jewish sensibilities are all the more offended, therefore, by the vicious and apparently gratuitous anti-Semitism which has come to expression among Negroes. The Negroes seem to be clipping the Jews in their glass jaw, to be saying that, despite their support for them, the Jew is still lowboy, still outside the pale, still declassed. It is a very effective way of telling the Jew he's colorless, not white, surely not black, just Jew. And the Jewish reaction seems to be an extension of what I can only clarify to myself as an experience of intensified grief, grief which covering six million is not yet deep or profound enough to cover the American Negro.

The frenzy of some sectors of American Jewish youth who

regard civil rights as the *only* issue of conscience in our time (leave aside for the moment Vietnam, which has all but ousted civil rights as the focus of personal agitation) has grown up with the dead of Europe long since buried and unknown. Their parents know but cannot really speak of it; for too many of them it is an unassimilated disaster for which no mode of expression and no order of psychic rationalization has been devised. They have not assimilated their own grief; they have nothing to transmit. Kids have a way of knowing where the unfilled "hole in being" is to be found and they have a marvelous capacity to put their finger in it, trace its circumference, and renew the bleeding. To be betrayed by the Negro is but one more link in the experience of having been betrayed by Europe. Try as he will to help, the help is finally rejected as unsuitable, unwanted, and the donor stands repudiated, slain in Europe, tormented here (and maybe some Jews think the black and white Christians will manage to compose their own hatred for each other long enough to do him in). I can't make this more precise (it's not fully clear to me what my own instinctive responses are telling me), but I do feel often a kind of weariness, lassitude, and sadness before this Negro anti-Semitism which I identify as one more moment in my own unexpressed, impounded grief.

It is possible, of course, that one reason for the American Jew's passionate support of the rights of the Negro comes from his desire to take a kind of revenge on Christendom, to take up those arms against the Christian ethos which he did not take up when his people were being destroyed in Europe. The Jew can't be passive twice in a generation. Slaughtered once, symbolically slaughtered a second time by the oppression of the Negro, there is a kind of ritual identification and horror that the slaughter should happen again. The Jew fights for the Negro because he fights for himself, not as white man, not as sharer in the experience of the Gentile, but as Jew. And what happens: his support is rejected; the Negro wants no part of the Jew. "But I'm not a white man, I'm a Jew," he replies. "White is white and white is Christian and you're *nothing*," he is told.

These are some of my thoughts about Negro anti-Semi-

tism. I have no program for combatting it. Others will have
programs. It doesn't shock me and it doesn't frighten. It
just makes me awfully god-damned sad.

JACOB COHEN

I OFTEN find myself speaking one way to Jews and quite
another way to non-Jews. And on "The Negro Question"
especially so. Speaking to Negroes about anti-Semitism, I
owe them what I owe the world, a firm sense of outrage, a
stubborn refusal to understand too well. With Jews, there are
fine distinctions to be made, *not for the Negro's sake*, but
for our possible use in coping with history, which repeats
itself, but not exactly. So at the risk of being overheard by
Negroes, in *Midstream*, let me make clear that in these
reflections I speak as a Jew to Jews.

According to a Negro saying, all white people are com-
prised of two parts: meanness and stinginess. The average
white man, runs the saying, is mostly mean: Jews are mostly
stingy. Now obviously this generalization is unfair to the
many Jews who have been incomparably generous to the
Negro Cause, and also to those of us who are mostly mean;
but then again such myths must help Negroes account for
those indubitably stingy Jews who cross their lives. Furthermore, side by side with this saying are many other Negro
sayings which cover us in our charitable, prophetic, and
martyrological incarnations. Several times at meetings in
Harlem I heard Malcolm X say some very violent things
about "Jewish slumlords," and then immediately, without
apparent irony, or noticeable protest from his audience,
urge Negroes to help themselves and respect themselves
"the way the Jews do." As always in Malcolm's expression,
and in traditional Negro expression, the analogy between
the Negro and Jewish plights was explicit. Therefore, while
I believe that no group in America is inclined to view us

under the aspect of one myth or another, I do not agree with the implication in the introductory statement to the symposium that these are all anti-Jewish myths, nor do I stress this out of Liberal habit.

There is no evidence of categorical, systematic anti-Semitism, of the Christian or racist variety, among Negroes, nor do any but a few exhibitionist black intellectuals like LeRoi Jones, who perform for the delectation of Jews in the audience, look upon the Jew as the quintessential white man. Action against Jews is part of the program of no known Negro organization or sect and there are hundreds of them, most of which have a membership no larger than their leadership. To be sure, "a large proportion of the businesses destroyed [in recent rioting] were Jewish owned" but to speak of these riots as "pogroms," as some of us have, leaves the inference that they were anti-Jewish in impetus, as if to say the riots would in some sense have not occurred, or there would have been less looting, if the storekeepers had not been Jewish—which of course is absurd. A pogrom needs Jews. Negro violence does not. A pogrom, by proper definition, takes place with the permission and often at the instigation of the police and administration and is in that sense an expression of the general will, even policy. But there is no evidence that the police failed to protect Jewish lives and property as best they could, which shows what an advantage it is for a Jew to be a white man in this country. The Negro is not a peasant as of old; he is an indifferent nativist, all efforts to incorporate him into a populist majority, including recent efforts, having failed. As the real anti-Semites in this country best know, the Negro has been and will be America's Jew, a fact, an historical condition, which fundamentally alters the situation of Jews in this country. I think in some part of themselves all Jews realize this, and, in very complicated variations, still feel kinship with the Negro cause.

Unquestionably, certain Negroes, many, are today uttering the word "Jew" in an increasingly violent manner, and many Jews are lashing back, but I don't think the conflict is *because* or *about* Negro attitudes toward the Jew or vice versa. The fact is that real-life Negroes and real-life Jews,

who for ancient reasons will inevitably call each other
"Jew!" or "Negro!", more and more are coming into objective conflict. Slum tenant and slumlord, customer and owner,
novice social worker and oldtimer, teacher and principal,
mailman and supervisor, integrationist and neighborhood
school defender—are very often Negro and Jew, and as
they collide, they do not pause to make meticulously fair
generalizations about the ultimate worth of each other's historical community.

Negroes have never learned that it is impolite to call a
Jew a Jew in public, perhaps because they are called
Negro so irrelevantly, so often.

Often there will be villainous remarks such as the now
famous comment by the former education chairman of the
Mount Vernon, New York, chapter of CORE, who said to
an opponent, an obstacle, whom he knew to be a Jew:
"Hitler should have killed more of you." A delirious, rotten
crack, worthy of no extenuating understanding, and prop-
erly rebuked by Mr. Will Maslow. But to me the remark is
significant only as proof that Negroes, too, know how to hurt
Jews when they want to. Mount Vernon's school problems
would be there even if all the resisters to integration in
town had been white Protestants, as they are in similarly
embattled towns, or if Mr. Brown had remained silent on the
subject of extermination. Some reprehensible forms of expression are coming into play, but it would be a mistake to suppose that the everyday conflict between Negroes and Jews
is caused, efficiently or finally, by anti-Semitism.

Jews and Negroes are in each other's way in cities throughout the country; there will be hard feelings, and I cannot
see how much can be done about it. The suggestion made
in the introduction that Jews be discouraged from opening
businesses in the ghetto cannot be taken seriously; no sound
businessman would want to invest in the ghetto—insurance
and mortgage rates are prohibitive, and the wild speculators
who will dart in and out to make a quick killing are not
likely to take advice from Jewish leaders. On the other
hand, it would be feasible and charitable to all concerned
to help some Jews get out of the ghetto. I know that many
small businessmen and slumlords would love to sell out if

they could find buyers, and I think some Jewish charitable
organization should buy Jewish-owned businesses and properties—there would be government money to help—and
then turn them over or sell them at reduced rates to responsible elements in the Negro community. Such a gesture would
meet the demands of the Black Power-ites at their face,
and it would get Jews out of harm's way. But I suggest
this as a possible gesture only, not as "a solution to the
problem"—there is none. Nor can I think of a Jewish organization which would entertain the notion, because it entails
singling Jews out in public, which our leaders never do.

If Jews and Negroes cannot (and should not) be taken
out of each other's way (short of apartheid) would some
"dialogue between their organizations" be useful? The question is, which organizations? The defense-type, community
relations organizations in the two communities—the NAACP
and Urban League; the AJC's and Anti-Defamation League
—share integrationist assumptions and genteel habits and
therefore as organizations could gain from each other's
company; but I have found that no Negro organization has
any constituents to deliver, so I don't think much will happen. Good-will parleys? By all means. They are nice.
Efforts to isolate and inhibit Mount Vernon-type incidents on
both sides, if they occur on both sides? All to the good.
Seminars in comparative suffering? No!

I am convinced that any attempt to achieve genuine rap-
port between Jewish and Negro organizations is futile, at
least presently, for two very different sets of rules govern the
public utterances of the two groups. From Negro leaders we
hear open protest and confessions of such intimacy concerning the pain and alleged impotence of Negro life that the
public would find them embarrassing coming from any other
group. Even the Black Power rhetoric—which attempts to
wrap Negroes in mystery—often becomes a form of self-
exposure, a new plot to gain that passionate surrender on
the part of white America which has been the goal of large
parts of the Civil Rights Movement. It is an apocalyptic
strategy, heading toward humiliation. And while Negro
spokesmen strut their anger and their hurt in public, Jewish
leaders are extremely circumspect in revealing the Jewish

heart of hearts. Protesting only stylishly, we confess nothing, guarding our privacy with attitudes of defense which are now almost inbred.

"The Negro Community" is not another ethnic community, for it lacks the passion for privacy which animates the other ethnic communities. I think Negroes could learn from our secretiveness, and we from their openness to America, but I don't see an organization in either community which could accomplish the exchange.

LUCY S. DAWIDOWICZ

WHEN I consider Negro-Jewish relations today, especially in the Civil Rights Movement, I am seized with a sense of *déjà vu*. It is like watching an old Russian movie about the 1870's, in black and white, with English subtitles.

A prominent psychologist (Negro) recently redefined anti-Semitism on a national-network television program. To hate Jews because you think they killed Christ is the rankest prejudice, he said, but to hate them because you believe they exploit Negroes is the sheerest objectivity. Alexander III, Emperor and Tsar of all Russia, also found such objective reasons to justify the pogroms of 1881: "The exploitation of the peasants by the Jews."

The crescendo of charges about "exploitation" by "Jewish merchants" and "Jew-landlords" grows precisely at a time when one would expect a diminuendo. Negroes are less dependent on local stores today than they used to be; their housing is better than it used to be, and the avenues of redress and repair are more numerous than they used to be. Also, though I do not have the quantitative evidence as proof,[1] I think that many Negroes who buy from local

[1] Preliminary data just released by the Anti-Defamation League of a study of Negro attitudes toward Jews appear to support my hypothesis.

merchants (Jews, Greeks, Puerto Ricans, or other Negroes)
and who live in substandard housing (owned by Jews,
Italians, anonymous banks, or other Negroes) think better
of their merchants and landlords than those who charge
exploitation but do not do business with the "exploiters."

No one loves a merchant and everyone abhors a landlord.
Proverbs abound in the folklore of every culture about the
cupidity and craftiness of buyers and sellers. The intellectuals, for once, share the folk's distrust. Thus, Emerson,
elegant and overrefined: "The ways of trade are grown
selfish to the borders of theft, and supple to the borders (if
not beyond the borders) of fraud." By now most city people
understand the nature of trade (the Romans knew it long
ago): that the buyer buys for as little as possible and the
seller sells for as much as possible. City people have learned
(perhaps too laggardly) that without trade the economy
would perish and that the distribution of goods is as vital
as their production.

Serfs and Populists

But peasants and revolutionaries have never regarded
business and trade this way. The anti-city, anti-money prejudices of the peasants were nourished by the anti-business,
anti-capitalist ideologies of the revolutionaries. Populists in
Russia made most headway among peasants not only with
agitation against the manor lords, not only with propaganda
against Emperor and Church, but also in arousing the peasants against the exploitation of merchants and innkeepers.

Negroes were America's serfs, today a landless peasantry
forced to seek work in the cities. Like the Russian serfs in
many respects, these poor Negro masses share with them
also a primitive religiosity embedded in superstition and a
distrust of urban mercantile society and of a money economy. Their leaders (some are only agitators), activists, militants, nationalists in the Civil Rights Movement, are
America's populists, articulating and escalating the latent and
patent prejudices of their masses, hoping to stir them out of
apathy into revolution. They are not pure demagogues:
many really believe in the demons they are exorcizing. In

1881, Narodnaya Volya, agrarian populists who embraced violence, applauded the pogroms in Russia as an unexpected revelation of the peasants' use of "revolutionary methods of struggle."

Stokely Carmichael and LeRoi Jones are America's Narodnaya Volya, preaching revolution, violence, and a species of economic anti-Semitism. (The distinction between power and violence eludes them.) *Vide* Stokely Carmichael:

> Black people do not want to "take over" this country. They don't want to "get whitey"; they just want to get him off their backs, as the saying goes. It was for example the exploitation by Jewish landlords and merchants which first created black resentment toward Jews—not Judaism.

Revolution or Counter-Revolution?

Such "ideas" make it hard to distinguish Black Power from Black Shirts or Black Hundreds. Pavolaki Krushevan wrote similar things in his paper in Kishinev for five years; then, in 1903, came the pogrom. LeRoi Jones says: "It is almost common knowledge that the Jews, etc., will go the next time there's a large 'disturbance,' like they say." (Last July, Jones was invited to Spelman College, of all places. His message—anti-Semitism, obscenity, revolution and violence. White students invite George Lincoln Rockwell to annoy their elders and amuse themselves; Negro students invite Jones and Carmichael to hear the Word from the minor prophets. Malcolm, of course, was the major prophet.)

The long-hot-summer looting and burning by Negroes of stores owned by whites, mostly Jews, have also been applauded as revolutionary outbursts. Bayard Rustin labeled the riots in Watts an "uprising," a "manifesto" the Negro masses issued to the white world. But consider how one Watts resident put it: "Then I came home and cats like me were having Christmas in August."[2]

In tsarist times, when word got around the villages that a

---

[2] Quoted in *SDS Bulletin*, IV, 2, 1965.

pogrom was being organized in town, the peasants hitched
the horses to the wagon to go for the loot. "Pogrom" is a
Russian word meaning riot, destruction, disturbance. (The
Jewish experience gave it a specific connotation: a riot
against Jews and Jewish property, with police and public
authorities failing to protect them.) Everybody but Jews
appreciated pogroms: the authorities because it diverted
peasant discontent, the agrarian populists because it stirred
the masses, and the peasants because it was Christmas in
August.

How does one distinguish between revolution and counter-
revolution? In Paris in 1789 the people stormed the Bastille;
in St. Petersburg in 1917 the people charged the prisons
and released the prisoners. Rioting, burning, looting may
be the occasional by-products of revolution, but they have
always been the essence of counter-revolution, initiated by
reactionary police, army, Black Hundreds, peasant mobs;
a successful way to dissipate revolutionary determination.

The Poor and the Margin of Profit

The poor do pay more. At the same time, notwithstanding
just grievances and malicious folklore that every Jewish
grocer drives a Cadillac and winters in Miami, merchants
in Negro neighborhoods earn less. In Harlem Jewish grocers
charge more than in Forest Hills; so do Greek grocers and
Safeway markets (if the chains can be induced to operate
there at all). Their expenses are higher (distributors and
accountants, for instance, are reluctant to serve these areas;
insurance, when obtainable, is costly, though no insurance is
costlier); risks are greater to property and even to life. Scar-
city of competition also keeps prices higher, a fact of capitalist
life in whose practice General Electric is much more adept
than the corner grocer. Except that at the corner the grocer is
accessible and, if he is a Jew, vulnerable, the object of familiar
prejudices. Still, the Jewish grocer gives credit, while A & P
and Safeway do not. The merchants recoup their losses from
bad credit risks by charging more, which is especially hard on
the poor. But the small merchants are without choice, for they
are themselves as much victims of the "system" as the poor.
Most make their living not just by compensatory high

prices, but by long hours, hard work, and in constant company with fear. Unlike the poor, they are unloved. Even when mugged or murdered, they are unpitied. In Chicago earlier this year, Negro "leaders" cheered the murder of two used-car dealers (Jews) and their salesman because they had charged high rates.

What is to be done about the poor? Some Negroes think the poor cannot afford a "middleman." Goods should go from producer directly to consumer, the middleman and his profit eliminated. (The same old utopias in new form.) Stokely Carmichael and LeRoi Jones have a "revolutionary" solution: expropriation. Naturally, without fair compensation.

Another "solution" is cooperation. How doth the Black Panther resemble the White Eagle. The anti-Semitic interbellum Polish government heavily subsidized consumer cooperatives to make room for the "native" *lumpen-petit-bourgeoisie*. Do Negro radicals realize how irrelevant the cooperative movement is in modern society? Even in Poland constant transfusions of government money did not make the cooperatives economically viable. In the United States the grocery cooperatives are the least successful of the not-very-successful cooperative movement. The margin of profit is much too small in the grocery business for the cooperative to be able to compete with the commercial enterprise.

If the poor are too poor to buy what they need, then they or the merchants must be subsidized. (I assume that we will not have a revolution and that businesses and real property will not be nationalized.) Frederick D. Sturdivant, who teaches marketing at the University of Southern California, suggested after surveying Watts that such Negro neighborhoods be treated like "certain undeveloped countries where risks of expropriation or destruction are abnormally high": State and Federal governments should guarantee capital investments of private companies to encourage them to do business in those neighborhoods. (We have already adopted rent subsidies to help the poor pay the landlord so that he can maintain the property with a margin of profit.)

Jewish Backlashers,
Cheek-Turners, Well-Spitters

Some Jews, reacting to the public eruption of Negro anti-Semitism in the Civil Rights Movement, stopped the money, especially to the organizations caught *in flagrante delicto.* This appeared to surprise the Negroes who expected the Jews to act like putative Christians and turn the other cheek. These Negroes seemed to equate the commitment to justice with an obligation to finance their movement. Meanwhile, back in the Democratic primary in Maryland last September, voters of Polish, Italian, German and Bohemian origin voted for a racist as their gubernatorial candidate, but Baltimore's Jews voted for the liberal who had supported the 1966 open-housing Civil Rights Bill. Thus the Jewish backlashers.

But there are also Jewish cheek-turners. They are chronically (or is it acutely?) embarrassed about being Jewish and they are ashamed of being associated with the uncouth Jewish grocer or the grasping marginal landlord. They insist that Negroes are not anti-Semitic, only anti-white. Their denial of the existence of Negro anti-Semitism is a sort of wish-fulfilling denial of Jewish corporate existence.

Finally, we have our alienated young and middle-aged Jews, spitting in the wells from which they drank. We have had them in every generation; there is nothing new under the sun. Nowadays they can be found among the boys and girls in Students for a Democratic Society, Northern Student Movement, white friends of SNCC and CORE, at the age when radicalism is still becoming to them. To some, Jews are their parents magnified and multiplied, the bourgeoisie, fat cats who have made it in the Establishment and the Power Structure. Like the young Jews in Russia's 1870's populist movement, today's radical Jewish youth may be providing their non-Jewish (Negro) comrades with the ideological rationalizations and psychological justifications for anti-Semitism.

"Chto delat?"

I would like to see Jewish organizations more insistent about the Negro responsibility to recognize anti-Semitism for what it is and repudiate it. Negroes are quick to tell us about Jews who are prejudiced against Negroes. To be sure. But such Jewish sentiments are not institutionalized and such private conversations are not public dialogues.

The Jewish community has, I believe, an obligation to help the Jewish shopkeepers in Negro neighborhoods who are victims of terror and violence. (And perhaps also some landlords—widows or pensioners whose livelihood derives from a return on the one or two units they own.) I have been told many merchants want to retire but cannot find buyers. Perhaps Jewish organizations that are training Negroes for business would bring the Jews and Negroes together and, with the help of the Small Business Administration, reach an equitable arrangement (not expropriation). Jews feel obligated to help a small Jewish community in a war zone in a far-off country; some merchants are in a war zone.

Our Jewish obligation is to do justly and in our universe of multiplicity there must be many self-respecting ways to do so besides contributing to Negro populists.

HOWARD FAST

THE PROBLEM of Negro anti-Semitism is neither simple, nor measurable. No one has ever done a scientific or even pseudo-scientific study of the state of anti-Semitism among the Negro People. The condition exists, but we can only speculate where and how much; and when it is articulated, it is shocking in terms of an ungainly horror. It is a strident, dreadfully wrong sound; and the response on the part of the Jewish listener is always a kind of sick confusion—a woeful protest that bolsters itself with logic, pleading that since the eighteen-twenties, here in America, the loudest and most consistently angry voice of protest against the Negro condition has been Jewish. (And here I do not for a moment

forget any of the Abolitionist movements, but refer to a continued record of unceasing, unslackening protest during a
century and a half.) Thus the knife not only cuts but twists
and ravages in the wound.

"Why?" the Jew pleads, asking for logic in a condition
of oppression that contains no logic. Yet the simple fact is
that the Negro by and large is a Christian, and anti-Semitism is a Christian way of life, a particular disease out of
a catalogue of diseases that have occupied the heartland of
Christian culture through history, such as reciprocal mass-
murder, bigotry, racism and other goodies, such as sexual
hypocrisy and unspeakable righteousness. To expect the
Negro to be free of this particular Christian habit would be
as unrealistic as it would be optimistic; to expect his condition of oppression to lessen this feeling would be even more
unrealistic. Quite to the contrary. If he sees his black skin
as a badge of shame, a mark of inferiority—and white
America has spared no effort to make this a part of the
Negro's psychology—then he will seek even more desperately
for what he may hate and regard as inferior.

I am well aware of the catalogue of reasons and sensible
explanations that have been offered to explain Negro anti-
Semitism. We are told that Jewish storekeepers in Negro
neighborhoods gouge the Negroes. (And so do Christian
storekeepers.) We are told of real estate owned by Jews in
ghettos. (But more is owned by Gentiles.) We are told that
Jews who work in Negro liberation organizations and give
of their lives to the Negro liberation struggle incur the
antagonism of those they attempt to help. (But thousands of
Gentiles work no better, no worse, in the same organizations.) We are offered psychological explanations as silly as
they are involved—and from all of it we emerge with the
same desperate sense of pain, that people to whom we hold
out a hand of help should—some of them—spit upon the
outstretched hand.

But all in all, we avoid the obvious explanation; for this
is the time of brotherhood, and if uncivilized hate-mongers
like Billy Graham go out to preach the gospel in support
of the war in Vietnam, we are not supposed to mention that
by and large Christianity has preached much the same gospel

for quite a while now. Jew and Gentile have clasped hands, haven't they? We are even off the hook, and the Vatican bears witness to the fact that we no longer carry a bag of guilt. But nobody seems to have watered this sudden change of attitude toward the Jew down to the grass roots. There are no tests, polls, public inquiries, but my own antennae sense a pretty fervent degree of anti-Semitism, all of it off the record. The Negro is dark-skinned, oppressed and used most murderously; he is also, with very few exceptions, a Christian, and when he enters his Church on Sunday, he shares in that world-wide white Christian benediction— anti-Semitism. And even if he never enters his church, he absorbs it by osmosis. Every force in the white world that surrounds him moves him to hate, and anti-Semitism is a Christian hate, practiced to perfection over two thousand years, handed to him ready made, as if the white world says to him,

"All other hates you must abjure—but this you may use. We approve your hatred of the Jew. We will applaud you and even support you."

But we want him to be noble enough to reject this useful, accepted white-Christian hate. We want him to say, "But the Jew is my friend and support and I will not hate him."

Very nice. But Negroes are people, no more, no less, and people are not noble unless they have been taught to be noble, and three hundred years of hate, slavery and oppression do not constitute a school for nobility.

There is anti-Semitism among Negroes because they are Christians in a Christian America, and because they are oppressed and desperate for anything that will enable them to fight against the white-American contention that they are less human. They strike out blindly where they may. The wonder is not in their striking out but in their marvelous restraint. And if among them there is anti-Semitism, this is less important in the human scheme of things than the enormous, over-all fact of their oppression.

MYRON M. FENSTER

THE JEWISH involvement in the struggle for Negro rights in this country and elsewhere is fraught with precariousness. There is no assurance that it will add stability or honor to either group. The Negro often resents it—and Jews often resist it. And yet—it must be done.

Involvement demands intricate but important choices. No one with a sense of responsibility or a capacity for reflection can just plunge in, flailing in all directions. The implications are many: What group does one join, which deserves financial support, with whom does one march and protest, how far does civil disobedience go before it descends into lawlessness—and altogether toward what goal is the Civil Rights Movement heading?

All this must be considered. And as one who thinks of himself as an activist, I would suggest that the voices of restraint must be considered as well, even if they are not in the end obeyed.

The reason for the latter is simply stated: As a Rabbi I must say quite candidly that the fight for Negro equality is only one of a half-dozen priority items to which my energies must be directed. To my way of thinking, it would be impossible to defer the others or cast them aside until this struggle is won. Some people are prepared to do so—just as there are some devoting full time to Jewish scholarship—and who am I to say that they are wrong. But, it is not likely that many of us are going to take their lead.

Since this is so, the Negro leadership will obviously have to carry the day and not only by default but by right. No one feels the heat of the fire as the one closest to it and no one is likely to move as rapidly. At the same time, for the Jews to remove themselves to the sidelines would be distressing not just for the Negro but for the Jewish community itself. One cannot sit out the major domestic revolution of our time, oblivious and secure. Besides, we must avoid an increasing tendency to retreat within our middle-class cloisters, counting and consolidating the gains of the last decades.

The Negro struggle may help the Jewish community from the danger of isolation and insularity. Equally, the Jewish role may be to help the Negro from retreating into a new black racism which must inevitably rear its head as anger, resentment and frustration of legitimate hopes ensues.

When the picket screams, "Black teachers for Black Harlem!" we must forcefully protest. Whenever extremism shows through we must patiently but consistently label it for what it is. But that is not enough. We must at the same time do whatever we can to see that exploitation and inequity of the Negro recedes. And how to keep at it in the face of disillusionment and setback is the key issue.

One of the main disillusionments is Negro anti-Semitism. That it is a problem can hardly be doubted. And to explain its origins as "traditional" Christian mores compounded by economic proximity in the ghetto does not dismiss or diminish its presence or lessen the pain of its sting. Naturally, responsible Negro leadership ought to—and does—denounce anti-Semitism. That it is not always easy to do so is part of the complex problem Negro leadership faces today, as they see the mobs swinging toward the extremists. Only when the responsible leaders will be able to show advances they have won (in jobs, housing, schools), will their hand be materially strengthened. And then they will be able to assert the most effective leadership.

In the meantime, simply to measure and record Negro anti-Semitism is a fairly fruitless pursuit. How helpful is it to learn that, given the choice, the Negro prefers the Jew over the white Christian, as a recent survey showed, when everyone knows that the tension between black and white today is such that each rejects the other?

Granted that the Jew may not be seen as an ally and that his participation in the "movement" is neither enthusiastically applauded nor gratefully acknowledged, does that diminish his responsibility or fundamentally alter his obligation? Is another repetition of the toughness of immigrant life on the East Side decades ago and how "we" pulled ourselves up

by those now immortal bootstraps really relevant? How
effective can such recitals be to the Negro who in the
1960's (not in the 'twenties or 'thirties) in the most affluent
country in the world finds himself economically unstable,
educationally outclassed, generally unwanted and trapped in
the ghetto with no visible way out?

By no reason of disillusionment can we exonerate our
disengagement. But there are other voices of caution that
would entice us and to which we must at least give ear. One
is that we Jews endanger our own security by concern for
and involvement in the struggle. That the backlashed Christian resents it and therefore the Jew will pay for it.

This fear has been flaunted in our faces before and
constantly. In the wake of its paralysis, the only response
possible would be to roll over and die. By virtue of such
fears Jews place themselves into a class of disembodied citizens, forever shivering in the face of Gentilism, outside the
stream of American aspirations and events. The truth is that
here as on almost every public issue, Jews differ among themselves. Those seeking activists will find them among the Jews
and there is no dearth of go-slowers and status-quoers.
Besides, when did those looking for mischief every find it
difficult to find? Are excuses for Jew-baiting needed for
those who seek them?

One other item of substance needs detain us. We Jews
today are a remnant people. If certain gains have been
made these past years and some newer trends have appeared,
they will not make up for the losses we have sustained. For
every family with some degree of Jewish identity or aspira-
tion there is at least one with none. No responsible Jewish
leader can constantly deploy the forces making for Jewish survival with abandon, caring little for the consequences
and unmindful of them.

Let me admit to feeling sad and cheated when some
marvelously idealistic college kid is ready to lay down his
young life to inch along the Negro struggle but would not
lift a pinky to save the whole Jewish enterprise from oblivion.
Some Jewish college kids have used the civil rights struggle
in a diversionary way, as some have used the peace movement. Limelight-drawing issues always run that risk though

it neither negates nor validates the issue which should be judged on its own merit. But the activists who fail to acknowledge the Jewish social idealism from which their convictions were nurtured and grew are not new either. Nor would they be likely to be in *shul* next Saturday in any case. Civil rights may not have saved souls for Judaism but it has not lost any either.

If Jewish identity is the argument, chances are more of our young people would be fascinated by the relevance and the dynamism of a faith that speaks to a burning contemporary problem than those chased by it. Hopefully, in the long run they will not be satisfied only with fruits but will search out the roots of their concern and involvement as well. Parenthetically, those who think that all Jewish college kids are high on civil rights ought to check their sources again. A new infatuation with "property rights" and individual prerogatives has smitten many of our campus crowd as anyone who has contact with them will report.

The question not beside the point then is this: Granted the anger and the extremism of the Negro today, what next? The popular reaction has been to backlash in the face of violence in the streets, to say in effect, let's see how far you guys can go on your own—surely you don't expect me to join the wild fist-swinging efforts. That is to say the mood today is to wash one's hands of the whole thing.

So then let us come to the heart of the matter. I see the Jews involved actively in the struggle for civil rights until it shall be won, to the very end, because it is right and proper, because it is wise and expedient.

At the risk of exercising preachment, the view that Judaism is not an heirloom to be lauded in rhetoric or paraded in passive reverential piety must be asserted. We see it standing relevant to this hour, its demands, judgements and texts not as decoration but as charges. Reading admonitions in sacred books to remember the stranger, not to stand idly by the blood of the neighbor, to sense the indignity of the worker not paid on time, or the feeling of the man from whom a pledge is to be collected, is to focus unconditionally on those in our midst who have not had their fair share of the blessings so many of us enjoy.

Who can turn away from the thousand daily slashes the Negro experiences? His manhood has been shattered and his hopes destroyed. In the South, they sometimes do it with hoses and dogs, in the North more subtly but no less painfully, by moving out when they move in, by refusing to send kids where they are, by getting scared near to death when anyone moves down the street. And in the Senate, they will not even bring to the floor a proposed law that at least in theory will make it possible for a Negro who has the cash to buy a house anywhere he wants, and a woman admittedly qualified will have to wait almost a year for endorsement as a federal judge solely because of color. Do we think that all of these things go unnoticed without welling up anger, hostility and extremism?

The Negro is caught today in the middle of a dilemma not of his own making. It can't come as any surprise in this post-Freudian era that people often become what we say they are. Tell a kid everyday that he is illegitimate and before long, like Edmund, he will be musing on bastardy. We want a responsible Negro community while we deny those conditions which alone can bring it into being.

We can't go on charging the Negro more for less, getting him deeper into garnisheed debt, let rats nibble at his kids' feet, send him to segregated schools—and if someone sells a house, worry, worry, start a rumor—a *schvartze* is coming —give him a job as a porter, make her always and only into a housemaid and then wonder why we can't have peace on our streets and in our homes.

Which leads to some words on expediency. We better wake up soon, I think to myself, before we have a revolution in every city in this country, which seems much less remote today than five years ago. By wake up I mean to stop this business about the civil rights talk being fine but I want life as usual, let someone else start because I'm not prejudiced and I've done my share. If we hope to save our society from interminable hostility we had better concentrate on a series of re-evaluated acts and attitudes on the part of all of us. No one is exempt. We are all involved.

Actually there are a number of very crucial areas where individual Jews and Jewish organizations with know-how can play a distinctive role. Acting as mediators, they can often negotiate between the aggrieved parties, respected and somewhat distrusted by both but all the time prodding toward progress without violence. In New York City in the education crises such a role has been played by an important Jewish group in efforts to bring aggrieved Negro parents and the education officials together if not in harmony at least toward a working arrangement.

The suburbs especially are going to become the scene of contested activity in the years ahead. Residential patterns will be challenged and violence may be imminent. To lead responsibly and affirmatively will be a crying need, and to prevent people from heading for the basement and closing down the hatch and appearing not to be at home when the hurricane comes. And through it all, if we expect rapid success or grateful recognition, we might as well forget it.

Is there a special Jewish stake in the Negro struggle? Not really. But we must make our people aware of the legitimate sources of Negro anger, disturb their complacency about slumlord-ism, over-charging and other abuses. And those of us impelled by ancient admonitions which we would make our own, are aware of the charge upon us not to play pattycake with abuses. We still consider ourselves under the obligation to burn out the evil in our midst. That does not obviate the obligation to choose wisely with whom and how we express our concern. But we are not free to desist from making the effort, nor can we afford to stand apart in silent spectatorism.

LESLIE A. FIEDLER

THIS IS A MOMENT for questions, new questions or old ones newly posed, a moment when answers seem impertinent—which is, perhaps, why fiction (a method of posing questions without troublesome question marks) seems the

most promising method of attacking the problem of Negro-
Jewish hostility. I am thinking of such books as Norman
Mailer's *An American Dream*, Nat Hentoff's *Call the
Keeper*, and Jay Neugeboren's *Big Man*, as well as (hopefully) my own *The Last Jew in America*. In a strange way
it has now become incumbent on the Jewish writer to
re-imagine the Negro in terms which will escape the old
WASP clichés, sentimental and vicious, and the recent even
more soupy and hysterical Spade ones. Eventually, of course,
the Negro writer himself will have to invent the New Negro
as Harriet Beecher Stowe, Mark Twain, D. W. Griffith
and Faulkner have invented the Old Negro. But Jews will
apparently have to deal with him in the moment of transition, since the current crop of Negro novelists is fumbling
the job: Ellison remaining stubbornly old-fashioned on this
score, Baldwin caught between the exigencies of his poetic
talent and his political commitment, LeRoi Jones the victim
of his own anguish and *mishigas*. But the Jewish writer's
assumption of this task can prove in the end only one more
possible source of misunderstanding and tension between the
two groups.

Some relevant questions then—and all which follows is a
series of questions even when passion or strategy leads me
to omit the question marks. Would not the proper title for an
article on this subject be "Thou shalt not honor the poor
man in his cause"—to remind the present-day enlightened
Jew of certain therapeutic anti-liberal elements in his own
tradition: a priestly admonition that might have protected
him in the 'thirties from illusions about the working class
and its parties (but did not); and might now serve as an
antidote against delusive hopes about Negroes and their
organizations (but probably will not). Or maybe it would
be better—in light of my own continuing concerns—to use
the title *An End to (Another) Innocence;* since the liberal
tradition in America—to which the Jewish intellectual has
attached himself, which, indeed, he has all but pre-empted—
insists on stumbling from one innocence to another with
appropriate bouts of self-recrimination between. It is not
mere "white backlash" (the very term is a buttress of
naivete on the defensive) but simple wisdom (what used to

be called "good sense") to notice that, like all such movements, the Civil Rights Movement is becoming, had to
become with the beginnings of success, self-seeking, self-
deceiving, self-defeating—devoted not to a search for justice
but to the pursuit of power. But the liberals (the *Jewish*
liberals, as Negro critics like to say) will be the last to admit
this; since the liberal is a man who can drown in the same
river twice—which is, let me be clear, his glory as well as
his folly, the function of an incredible generosity of spirit
which fades imperceptibly into willful stupidity: a combination, mythologically speaking, of *yiddishe hartz* and *goyishe
kop.*

Why not continue to speak mythologically then; for mythology seems the basic way into the problem of Jewish-Negro
hostility—which turns out not to exist sociologically at all,
i.e., not *consciously* (using the methods of the behavioral
sciences, investigators keep discovering to their own satisfac-
tion and the confusion of the rest of us, that Negroes really
love, respect and honor Jews) but only pre-consciously, on
the level of legend and nightmare.

What in fact, are the mythologies at work, first in the
minds of Negroes concerning Jews and then in the minds
of Jews concerning Negroes? "Sub-minds" would be a more
precise way of naming the locus of myths: and is it not well
to remind ourselves in this regard of the differing weights of
mind and sub-mind, conscious and preconscious factors in
the case of Negro and Jew? It is no secret, surely, that in
America the Jewish Community has largely committed itself
to a life of logos, a cultivation of the ego and the whole
Gutenburg bit whose demise Marshall MacLuhan has been
quite un-Jewishly predicting; while the Negro community in
large part continues to live (even to make its living) in the
world of sub-literacy, unrationalized impulse, and free fantasy.

Do not Negroes, in any event, tend to begin with the
WASP racist mythology (endorsing it in self-hatred, or
inverting it in impotent rebellion) which divides the world
into two ethnic-mythic segments only: White and Colored;
and which further assumes that the distinction is hierarchal,
corresponding roughly to higher and lower. The deep Jewish

ethnic-mythic division, on the other hand, is threefold, as
the legend of the three sons of Noah reminds us. As descendants of Shem, we were once taught, we have *two* hostile and
inferior brothers, Ham and Japheth. The Negro, committed
to his simpler mythology, tends to regard the Jew either as
a Colored Man who is deviously passing as White; or a
goddamned White Man pretending, for reasons hard to
fathom, to the fate of the excluded Colored Man. The Jew,
meanwhile, is struggling with the vestigial sense of being a
third thing, neither-either, however one says it; and he therefore thinks of himself (his kind of awareness driving him
compulsively from feeling to thinking) of being free to "pass"
in either direction, in a world which oddly insists that he
identify himself with one group of strangers or another,
Hamitic or Japhetic. And he knows that historically segments
of his people have done both (some first pretending to be
White, then becoming prisoners of their pretense; some following the opposite strategy): that in Israel, for instance, it
is possible to observe these two groups, "Black Jews" and
"White Jews," in open conflict. He is, therefore, baffled as
well as resentful when he discovers himself denominated
"White" without choice and made the victim in a Black-
White race riot; just as he was once baffled as well as resentful to discover himself linked without choice to Negroes in
being excluded from White clubs and hotels and restau-
rants. And he is doubly baffled and resentful when the
Negro switches from hating him as White to despising him in
a mode imitated from those earlier-arrived North European
Americans, who thought themselves so much Whiter than he.

How can the Jew not help seeing Negro anti-Semitism as
a kind of culture-climbing, an illegitimate attempt to emulate WASP style—and, inevitably, a belated and misguided
attempt; since the WASPs are abandoning the racist attitudes to which the Negro aspires at the very moment he
is assimilating them. Even Hitler, certain more ignorant
or frantic Negroes tend to think of as just another White
Man—rather more efficient than most, though not quite
efficient enough in eliminating his Jew-enemies—and thus
they have not felt shamed out of their anti-Semitism by the
rise and fall of Nazism, as their WASP opposite numbers

(who cannot help feeling Hitler in some sense one of them) have tended to be. It is especially unassimilated, unassimilable Jews, Jews who do not even seem to want to look like all other Americans, who stir the fury of Negro hoods—say, Hasidim with their beards, *peyes* and gabardines.

At the deepest mythological level, is it not the Jewish religion, finally, as well as the Jewish ethnic inheritance which bugs the Negroes? Certainly this would be understandable enough; for insofar as they are Christians, fundamentalist, evangelical Protestants, do they not inherit the simple-minded anti-Jewish mythology of the Gospels (which Catholics long had the good grace to keep out of the hands of subliterates) with its simple-minded melodrama of "our" Christ killed by "the Jews"? And do not Negroes in particular possess the additional sentimental myth of Simon the Cyrenean—kindly Negro by the wayside—who helped Jesus bear his cross as the Jews hooted and howled for his blood? And insofar as they are becoming Muslim (Why could not the first attempt of the ill-fated founder of that movement to establish a Black Judaism have succeeded?), are they not obsessed by the legendary notion of the "Evil Jacob," Israel the Usurper—as well as the myth of Isaac before him doing poor Ishmael out of his heritage? And as Muslims, do not they (along with the members of other non-Mohammedan Afro organizations) identify themselves with an Arab-African anti-Jewish political mythology, which leads them to consider Jews, in America as well as Israel, even wickeder than the rest of the depraved "hoojis"? Are not both Christianity and Islam, finally, being offshoots of a more primitive Judaism, subject to spasms of a kind of collective sibling rivalry, which passes over on occasion into fratricidal strife? And is not the *shul*-goer or temple-attending Jew caught once more in the old bind between the Christian Negro for whom he is not (spiritually) White enough—not sufficiently washed in the Blood of the Lamb—and the Muslim Negro for whom he is not (mythologically) Black enough—not far enough removed from the White Man's God?

It is not, however, only the worshippers of Christ or the followers of Mohammed among the Negroes who are pos-

sessed by anti-Jewish mythologies. The hippiest and most
advanced Negroes, secular as they may seem to themselves,
are committed to a myth system—the Beat Religion, let's
call it for the purposes of quick identification, most recent
form of an old Romantic anti-Church. And does that Church
not necessarily, in view of its archetypal antecedents, see
the Negro as the embodiment of (admired) impulse and
irrationality, the Jew as the incarnation of (despised) subli-
mation and rationality? About these matters I have written
at some length before; and have thought about them long
enough not to be surprised at recent efforts at expelling Allen
Ginsberg from the True Church (a kind of apostle to the
Beat Gentiles, or maybe better, a Trotsky of the Hip revolution—his position is more than a little anomalous). No
one, at any rate, need pretend astonishment when he hears
the cry from a Negro at the back of a room in which Robert
Creeley is reading aloud, "This is a poem for Allen Ginsberg"—"Hey, man, when you going to stop talking about
those Jew poets?" Is it not a rule of the mythological literary life in America that when the Negro is up, the Jew is
down? What was true in the 'twenties, is true once again as
the Jewish 'thirties, 'forties and early 'fifties recede from us.
Who can serve two masters, after all? One must choose
between Saul Bellow and LeRoi Jones, Jerusalem (well,
the Northwest side of Chicago at any rate) and Harlem
(well, let's make it Newark's Third Ward). Mythological as
well as historical factors, that is to say, have determined
the fact that certain Hippies at the present moment find
themselves protesting a Jewish Literary Establishment
("Norman Podhoretz's floating ghetto," one in-group joke
calls it) in the name of a movement whose reigning figures
are archetypal *goyim* like Charles Olson, Norman O.
Brown and Marshall MacLuhan. Jewish writers, from Mailer
to Nat Hentoff, may try to escape the mythological hang-up
by redefining themselves as imaginary or "White Negroes"
(the very term was, of course, invented by a Jew)—just as
their more political brethren have tried to assimilate to a
world which mythologically rejects them by linking arms
with Negroes in protests and demonstrations. But though
young Jews have an affinity not only for protest but for

folksongs, jazz and marijuana (how much more readily they assimilate to pot than to the Paleface medicine of whiskey), the whole syndrome, they have trouble making it across the legendary line—remain always in danger of being told that they cannot *really* commit themselves to the Movement, cannot *really* make authentic jazz, cannot *really* sing the blues. The point is that other mythological demands are being made on them—to play the false liberal, or "Mr. Goldberg" or, ultimately, the super-ego in one or another currently unfashionable form.

So much—for the moment—about the Negro or Negroizing mythologies of the Jew; though I suppose a word at least demands to be said about the "Black Socialism" (the term antedates its adoption by actual Blacks), that presumably revolutionary anti-Semitism which poor Negroes have inherited from White workers, *lumpen* proletarians, peasants and "red-necks." This view (to which Leo Franks was once a victim) sees the Jew as rich, powerful, devious, behind the scenes if not at the centers of power—a Boss, in short. But this view tends to become less and less influential as the leading elements of the Negro Movement become prosperous or mobile and educated enough to afford overt anti-Semitism. It is real enough, to be sure, but is it not finally a vestige, as old-fashioned, which is to say, as peripheral in the current situation as the remnants among the aging Jewish bourgeoisie of the simple-minded anti-Negroism appropriate to our social-climbing days: the contempt of the still insecure Jewish housewife for the *schwarze* who cleaned for her, or the Jewish marginal small businessman for his Negro janitor, or the underpaid Jewish salesman for his Negro instalment customer? Do we not enjoy rehashing such elementary prejudices, long after we have made it in a way which renders them irrelevant, precisely because they are no longer urgent; and leaving them, we would have to confront relationships much more difficult to analyze or confess?

Almost as familiar, and therefore quite as ritually satisfying to discuss yet one more time are certain good old Freudian notions—long since lapsed into semi-popular mythology—about the Negro: the projection onto the Negro

male, for instance, of the sadist nightmares about his own
women dreamed by the white male etc. etc. These have
always been rather confused as far as Jews in America are
concerned, by the fact that Jews themselves have played
similar mythological-sexual roles in WASP erotic fantasies;
and in Norman Mailer's last novel one can see enacted in
the form of comic melodrama a kind of contest between his
(half) Jewish hero and a particularly potent Spade to see
which one will possess the blond all-American *shikse*—which,
mythologically speaking, amounts, I suppose, to an argument about which one of us she is dreaming these days.
More interesting, and more dangerous to broach, are questions about the role of homosexual rather than heterosexual
fantasies in the earlier stages of the Civil Rights Movement.
I am not referring to the fact that there has been a strange
confluence of the Homosexual Rebellion (the emergence of
queer America from underground to the daylight world)
and the Negro Movement; but rather to the influence on
that Movement of the old anti-female dream of a pure love
between males, colored and white, so crucial to our classic
literature in the United States. I myself can report having
heard several times in various forms from young civil rights
workers the cry, so authentically American it was hard at
first to believe: "Oh, Christ, things were great when just us
buddies black and white were fighting it out together; but
these White chicks are just down here to get laid."

It seems to me, however, that none of these sexual concerns, deep as they may go, are as important at the moment
as certain political mythologies. What chiefly exacerbates
relations between Negroes and Jews, as far as Jews are
concerned, is the persistence among them of the mythology
of Liberal Humanism. This troublesome myth-system, derived
in part from Old Testament sources, most highly developed
in modern Anglo-Saxondom, and picked up again in that
world by emancipated Jewish intellectuals, includes the following articles of faith: that all men desire freedom and full
human status and deny that freedom and status to others
only when it has been refused to them; that equality of
opportunity leads to maximum self-fulfillment and social well-
being; that the oppressed and the injured have been so

ennobled by their oppression and injury that they are morally superior to their masters; that all men desire literacy and suffrage—and can exercise those privileges equally well when granted them; that all the foregoing are not the parochial belief of a tiny minority of mankind over a minute span of time, but what all men have always believed, or would have believed given the opportunity. Intertwined with this credo—though not as often avowed as that credo itself— is the Whig Myth of History which sees freedom slowly broadening down from precedent to precedent, country to country and ethnic group to ethnic group. The Jews have always (since their exit from the ghetto and entry into the West at least) considered themselves more qualified than anyone, less compromised than anyone because of their historical situation certainly, to preach this doctrine. They have felt especially righteous in respect to the application of these principles to the Negroes in the United States, since they were not as a group involved in the enslavement of the Negro, and they know themselves to have long been involved in Civil Rights Movements in numbers all out of proportion to the percentage of the total population which they represent. No Negro ever died for a Jewish cause, Jews tell themselves; but some of our boys have died for Negro rights.

How utterly unprepared they have been, therefore, to find a growing number of Negroes rejecting not only their credo but them in particular as its messengers—spurning in short the whole body of "Jewish Liberalism." "Hear our message and be saved," they cry only a little condescendingly, and are dismayed to hear in return: "All we want from you white mothers (or alternatively, Jew mothers) is to get off our backs and out of our road!" Yet worse, much worse, is the fact that the Negroes, whatever their avowed credo, challenge by their very existence a basic article of the Liberal Faith: equality of opportunity will not grant very many of them, brutalized by long brainwashing and bred by a kind of unnatural selection, a decent life or the possibility of prosperity. What they demand, not so much by what they say as by how they are, how they test, how they perform, is *special privilege* rather than equality if they are to make it at all in the very world in which the Jews have so pre-

eminently flourished. And what a shame and embarrass-
ment that some men (i.e., most Jews) have done so well
under conditions in which certain fellow-humans seem
bound to do ill. What can survive of liberal mythology in
the face of this? Is "liberalism," then, only a camouflage
for a special sort of privilege, a code by which the peoples
who alone have long lived with the alphabet can triumph
over all others?

Marxism, especially in its more brutal Bolshevik versions,
has long offered an alternative mythology to that of liberalism; but so many intellectual Jews now sufficiently advanced
into middle age to have become its spokesmen have been
there before. Some, indeed, are alive and articulate at
the moment who have lived through the loss of three religions: first Orthodoxy itself, then Stalinism or Trotskyism,
finally enlightened liberalism; and for them, what lies ahead
but despair? But for the young, and the politically obtuse
who remember nothing and have learned nothing, it seems
possible, even imperative—in order to justify or explain
black violence, black know-nothingism, black racism—to
fall back once more on the mythology of an already once-
discredited anti-liberal Bolshevik "Humanism." Certainly,
there is superficial reassurance at least in the simple-minded
theory that the whole vexed problem is "economic"—and
that the last vestiges of Black Racism will disappear (like
anti-Semitism in the Soviet Union? a nagging voice
demands) only after the major means of production have
been appropriated by the People's State. But how can a
thinking man live by the mythology of a God who died in
the declining 'thirties? And how especially can a Jew come
to terms with the fate of his own people by applying a Marx-
ist mythology which denies the Jewishness of the Jews—as
is, after all, appropriate to a secular religion invented in
large part by recusant Jews. To be sure, any and all "Jewish
problems" immediately disappear when the real reference
of the adjective is denied; but this is a semantic solution
which cannot conceal the fact that actual Jews are being
harried and threatened. And if proof is needed that this
semantic strategy is not only a lie but an offense, one need
only see Peter Weiss' current play, *The Investigation*, that

obscene parody of what happened at Auschwitz, from which
"the Jews" have been expunged, even as a name to be
spoken aloud.

No, more attractive to me than yesterday's defunct mythology—more valid for all the self-pity easily attached to it
—is the more ancient mythology which insists that the ultimate villains of history define themselves finally and essentially by their attitude toward the Jews; and that all enemies
of the Jews (with whatever pious slogans and whatever
history of suffering they begin) are enemies to the good of
mankind, whether they be black, brown, yellow or white—
Haman or Hitler or the CORE leader rising to scream that
Hitler should have done a better job of getting rid of us.
"Not in one generation alone, but in every generation they
have risen up to destroy us," the ritual phrase in the Passover
Haggadah runs; and it continues on to reassure us that God
has always delivered us out of the hands of our enemies.
But what about the hands of our presumed, even our real,
allies? And what can we expect anyhow in these dark days
when God is dead and only the devil survives: the devil still
identified by Ku Kluxers with Negroes, and by some Negroes
with the Jews? What does the devil's devil do in a world
without God, or even gods?

Despair? Make jokes? Pray to the void? Confess that
nothing can be done? That by a joke of history the amends
that *must* be made to the Negroes (for indignities for which
the Jews bear little or no guilt) must, alas, necessarily do
harm to the Jews? That it is our turn again, or really on
this continent, at long last? Sometimes I feel this way and
am tempted toward desolation; until, looking out into the
streets, the schoolyards, the coffeehouses, I find my heart
leaping up at the sight of young couples linked arm in arm.
And I think our daughters will save us, love (not big theo-
retical, but small sexual love) will save us. I remember a
year or two ago riding a plane to Jerusalem and being told
by the man seated beside me, who worked for a Jewish
adoption agency, that the number of illegitimate Negro
babies being produced by Jewish girls was mounting spec-
tacularly. And were there also, I asked, legitimate ones,
even legitimate ones? But I did not listen for the answer,

knowing it was yes, and not quite sure why I needed confirmation. What sunders us may not be first of all but is last
of all a sexual taboo; and that taboo is every day being
broken, with or without benefit of clergy, Christian or
Jewish; and its breaking is the beginning (though *only* the
beginning) of the end.

So naturally a new mythology is being invented, appropriate to that new solution; though like all new myths this
one, too, contains within it one very old, indeed, the myth
of the Jewish Daughter, Hadassah (renamed Esther, which
is to say, Ashtoreth) dancing naked for our salvation before
the Gentile King. I sat the other day eavesdropping on the
conversation of a group of very young white girls—most of
them pretty, blonde daughters of Jews with black boyfriends,
discussing what they would do when the first race riots broke
out in Buffalo. And one of them suggested that they march
between the two opposed packs, Black and White, carrying
signs which read: MAKE LOVE NOT WAR. It was elegant
and vain as the loveliest dream; and I am old and cynical
enough, after all, to know it; as I know how much there
is dark and desperate even in their young love, and as I
realize how much in marriage itself (for some few of them
will marry their Negro boyfriends, I am sure) is a problem
rather than a solution. To make matters worse, I had just
been reading in the *East Village Other* a statement by a
Negro poet, who not so long before had been able to write
that he had "married a Jewish Lady to escape Bohemia,"
that Jewish girls only married Negroes in order to emasculate
them. And I was aware that it was his paranoid and sinister
mythology which operated in the tensions that made headlines day after day; but I knew that the counter-mythology
of those young girls had power to move men, too. I, at least,
prefer to live in its hope rather than the Negro poet's despair,
convinced of its superiority to all the weary mythologies of
mere politics. The disillusionment it will inevitably breed at
least still lies ahead, and (if I am lucky) I may not live so long.

ROLAND B. GITTELSOHN

NO TWO segments of the American population are in some respects so close, in others so removed and remote, as are Negroes and Jews. Both were in the beginning immigrant groups, coming to these shores in substantial numbers only after the first foundations of an American nation had been laid. Both are predominantly urban in residence. Both reached the point of bursting through narrow neighborhood walls, pushing impatiently into areas which had previously been closed to them. Both have been numerically insignificant and oppressed minorities, religiously-motivated in their struggle for self-expression and emancipation. Both have suffered similar internal stresses between the forces of survival and those of assimilation and escape.

Yet the differences are no less profound. Jews came to America because they wanted to—freely, hopefully, passionately. Negroes first set foot on this soil as captive slaves. Jews brought with them a sophisticated tradition and culture. Negroes are rootless and lost, divorced from the civilization to which they had been indigenous, rudely excluded from that which was emerging here. Jews have improved themselves economically to the point where there is virtually no Jewish proletariat left. Negroes—despite some progress in recent years—remain mostly restricted to menial and unskilled employment. Jews have played an increasingly important role in the political development of the nation. Negroes have barely begun even to sense their potential as a political force. It would be a gross misreading of history to assume simply that Negroes are behind Jews on a timetable which is destined to bring them to the same goals, albeit several generations later. Many of the differences are qualitative and substantive; we shall have occasion to see that in some detail shortly.

Perhaps it is this paradox, this simultaneous similarity

and divergence between Negro and Jew in America, which
can help us understand the intensity of the relationship
between them today. The first prerequisite, if any meaningful kind of progress is to be achieved, is that we face facts.
That is to say, facts as they are, not as we might like them
to be or as some of our agencies of protection and propaganda imagine them to be.

The most dominant and inescapable fact is that considerable antagonism exists in both directions, that substantial
anti-Semitism is to be found among Negroes, while strains
of anti-Negro prejudice are discernible among Jews. Nothing
is to be gained by attempting to deny the truth. A New York
study made as long ago as 1946 revealed that 60 percent
of the Jews queried held unfavorable stereotypes regarding
Negroes, while 70 percent of the Negroes disclosed similar
stereotypes about Jews. It can be reasonably assumed that
any change in the last twenty years has not been for the
better.

The perceptible growth of anti-Semitism in the Negro community can be understood on several grounds. Many com-
mentators have already called attention to the fact that for
most American Negroes the Jew happens to be the most
proximate white man. Of all whites, he is most often present
and visible—either as local merchant or as landlord. He is
therefore the most immediately available target for whatever
diffused resentment is felt against white people generally.
This is true but it is far from a complete explanation. At
least two additional factors contribute to the special viru-
lence of anti-Jewish sentiment among Negroes.

The first is the fact that anti-Semitism is perhaps the only
sociological phenomenon through which the Negro can identify with the white majority, can himself become part of
the dominant social sector by which he is ordinarily excluded
and victimized. By virtue of his black rather than white
skin, the Negro feels inferior. By virtue of his Christian
rather than Jewish faith, in a predominantly Christian nation
he acquires an illusion of superiority. Not that a psychological
process so subtle as this is actually articulated. But the
very fact of its being unconscious makes it more operative
and insidious.

A second factor—too often either ignored or minimized—
emerges from the theological rather than the psychological
component of the Negro's religious identification. Most dark-
skinned Americans have been not only Christians, but
adherents of one or another of the fundamentalist sects.
They have thus been inclined to accept a literal, not a liberal
interpretation of those Christian doctrines which have been
so troublesome as seminal causes of anti-Semitism: that
Jews as such killed Christ . . . that they were therefore
rejected by God as an accursed people . . . that they are
condemned to wander homelessly until they agree to accept
Christian dogma. It is too early to assess the effect on
Negro anti-Semitism either of the Black Muslim movement
or of the tendency within Christendom to mitigate the old
libels against Judaism and the Jews. Even if our expectations
from these developments be sanguine, however, the fact
remains that most Negroes with whom we deal today are
products of a Christian creed which induces them toward
anti-Semitism. Thus psychological and theological motives
conspire to encourage antagonism on the part of Christian
Negroes against American Jews.

Now what of anti-Negro prejudice among Jews? It too
exists, and it can be explained on several levels. At its crud-
est, it was expressed to me thirty-five years ago by a Jew who
was notable neither for intelligence nor sensitivity. He said:
"The more prejudice exists in this country against the blacks,
the safer we Jews will be. *They* are a lightning-rod for our
protection." It should be observed at once that such protection is illusory and that only an infinitesimal number of
Jews in America today harbor such ridiculous notions. Nor
should it be forgotten that we Jews have a long history of
relatively favorable attitudes and actions toward the Negro
minority. More than two decades ago Gordon Allport sum-
marized his own investigations and those of others, by writ-
ing: ". . . studies of prejudice show that the average Jewish
attitude seems to be significantly more tolerant than the
average attitude in Catholic or Protestant groups."[1]

The record should not be falsified in either direction. We

---

[1] G. Allport: *The Nature of Prejudice*, p. 125. Beacon Press, 1954.

have done more than others to correct injustice to the Negro, but we have not done enough. Honesty compels us to confess that prejudice does serve certain psychological functions, even if pathologically. It enables the person who feels—and, indeed, perhaps who is—inferior in every other way to achieve a spurious status vis-à-vis someone who is even less prestigious in his eyes than himself. Shakespeare was scarcely the first to observe that Jews are human beings, like all other human beings, with similar eyes, ears, wants, fears, hopes and emotional imbalances. The same mechanisms of frustration and compensation which operate within other men are to be found in us. In our long, lugubrious history we have not often been able to indulge in the luxury of sublimating our own pains by directing hostility against others. For the most part, we still eschew such cheap psychological satisfactions. But it would be idle to deny that there are some in our midst who have taken refuge in an anti-Negro stance from the inadequacies and disadvantages they would otherwise find it difficult to acknowledge. We have already observed that for many Negroes the Jew is the only white man against whom he can vent hostility without fear of paying too extravagant a penalty. By the reverse of the very same psychology, there are some Jews who can with impunity voice their resentment of all Christians only against the most helpless of them in this country, Negroes.

This is apt especially to be true among those lower-middle-class Jews who live in areas which have either already been largely taken over for Negro occupancy or are immediately contiguous to such areas. Their attitudes are not too unlike those of other immigrant groups—the Irish, Poles, Italians, et al—who inhabit similar neighborhoods. They are the ones against whom the expansion of Negro rights poses the greatest threat, in terms both of physical proximity and of social status.

So we have both latent and overt prejudice in each group against the other; and we have at least some little understanding of the dynamics which are responsible for such prejudice. Which brings us to the real heart of the matter: what kind of program can be projected for dealing with the situation as it in fact exists?

Let us Jews begin on the most elementary level of admit-
ting that there are Jewish slumlords and unscrupulous merchants. The facts that most Jewish owners of property and
business in the Negro ghetto are decent and honest . . . that
there are more Gentile than Jewish landlords who abuse
their tenants . . . that, indeed, some Negro owners are
among the very worst offenders: none of these patent truths
should be permitted to camouflage or obscure those Jews
whose behavior toward Negro tenants or customers leaves
much to be desired. Such Jews are the responsibility of the
entire Jewish community. In the absence of operative communal authority, they will not be easy to control or even to
influence, but this difficulty does not exonerate us from the
effort. Individual Jews who are remiss in these respects must
be confronted by their rabbis, by the officers of Jewish
Community Councils and Federations, by their peers in the
country clubs to which they belong—in short, by any and
every authority-figure in the Jewish community who could
conceivably bring pressure to bear. And yes, why not learn
a lesson from our fund-raising experts? Let them be
approached if necessary also by those on whom they are
economically dependent!

Will such action, even if it be successful, substantially
alleviate Negro anti-Semitism? It should have some effect. I
would guess that the mere knowledge among Negroes that
the Jewish community is moving along this line would be
impressive and effective. But the most efficacious use of
communal discipline will probably make no more than minor
inroads on the incidence of anti-Semitism. Our own defense,
however important it be to us and the community, is not the
most persuasive motive for the program here recommended.
We need to embark upon such action not in terms of a
quid-pro-quo but, plainly and simply, because it is right! To
be a Jew must mean to stand for righteousness and justice
even if our short-run interests were thereby to suffer.

Some Jews are fond of holding up to the Negro—either
in chastisement or challenge—our own example of self-help.
The implication is: if we could lift ourselves up so drama-
tically in two or three generations by our own bootstraps, why
can't you do the same? The parallel is spurious; the induce-

ment is insulting. We have already observed that we came
here willingly while the Negro was dragged here in chains.
Also that we brought with us a millennial book culture, a
portable civilization which could easily be transported with
us from one continent to another. We therefore did not start
from scratch. The culture to which the Negro was accustomed before being forcefully imported to the United States
was not the kind that could be carried along. Here he had
to commence with nothing of his own that might provide him
either with compensation or goad. The Negro today, moreover, is struggling for advancement in an economy whose
unskilled sector is contracting under the impact of automa-
tion; he lacks the advantage we had of getting his initial start
in an expanding frontier economy which opened up considerable opportunity for advancement even at its less lucra-
tive edges.

It should be observed here, at least parenthetically, that
when the Negro takes seriously the example of self-help held
before him, with the result that he seems to be withdrawing
from the white world and resorting to what some have
dubbed Black Power, the very people who have challenged
him in this respect are often among his first and most
vociferous critics.

Both Negroes and Jews must be reminded that their
causes are ultimately indivisible. It is a truism that a society
which is unstable or unsafe for either will be at best precarious for both. In his fascinating study of the Beiliss case,[2]
Maurice Samuel reminds us of how easy it has always been
for an evil power structure to delude its victims by diverting
their attention to a helpless minority. Both Negro and Jew
have played this tragic role in history. What a miserable
shame it would be now for either to be trapped into using
the other as a decoy, instead of uniting our efforts and zeal to
build the only kind of society in which both can be secure.

Have I made it appear that only we Jews are obliged to
change some of our ways? This would obviously be neither
accurate nor fair. The main thrust of my argument has been
aimed in that direction simply because I am addressing an

[2] *Blood Accusation;* Alfred A. Knopf, 1966.

audience which can be assumed to be mostly Jewish. No use in dwelling for them on what others should be doing.

The American Negro does face inescapable obligations; of course he does. The final paragraph in the foregoing section is no less applicable to him than to us. He is, moreover, the only one who can analyze and, as a consequence, significantly remedy those psychological and theological distortions which may predispose him to anti-Semitism. In addition, if there is to be continuing and meaningful dialogue between him and ourselves, he must take steps to establish a responsible Negro community with identifiable leaders. As disorganized and elusive as our own community may be, for understandable historic reasons the Negro community is often non-existent. In Boston there have been occasions when we Jews have been utterly frustrated in attempting to locate our Negro counterparts for honest confrontation.

Both Negro and Jew need to learn more about each other and about their respective histories. It would be particularly constructive for the Negro to know more about Israel's contribution to the development of the African nations, especially since he is now becoming more aware of his own cultural affinity with them. We can supply the necessary information, but the actual instruction—if it is to be effective and beyond suspicion of ulterior motive—must be given to Negroes by Negroes.

Finally, responsible Negro leadership has the same obligation to discipline and disavow the anti-Semites in their group as we have to deal harshly with racists among ourselves. There is no room for repetition of the reluctance and reservation with which the national office of CORE repudiated a vicious expression of prejudice by one of its Westchester County leaders last spring.

But in the end, for a Jew addressing other Jews, our own responsibility takes precedence. To be a Jew means to be a special kind of human being, a kind committed under all circumstances to the pursuit of justice. Our dedication to what is right must be unconditional. It cannot be contingent on reciprocity. Either the chosenness of which tradition speaks means this, or it means nothing.

There will be more than a few setbacks along the way,

momentary disappointments and defeats which may discourage both groups. We must expect them but not be crushed by them. The relationship between these two minorities—so similar, yet so agonizingly different—will for some time yet be the focal point of pain in America's struggle to locate its soul. If neither Negro nor Jew expects perfection of the other, if both will concentrate on what they share in common, if they will keep their ultimate goals always uppermost, the day can and surely will be won.

JACOB GLATSTEIN

WHEN ONE observes the recent events in Grenada, Mississippi where white hooligans brutally assaulted Negro children while the "Law" stood by and watched and did not interfere; when one considers that these children were participants in action that would raise—be it ever so little—the prestige of America in the eyes of the world, while the guardians of the "Law" degraded America before all mankind, one is inclined to feel that all symposia are futile, that it is a waste of time to talk and to debate, that only action, action, action is the order of the day.

Nevertheless we are conscious that we live in a world of cruel possibilities; that during the past quarter century we have witnessed the brutalization of entire nations—the Germans, the Indonesians, the Chinese, the whites in South Africa; we are overwhelmed with a sense of helplessness and we revert to the "tested weapon" of talk; we do not remain silent, instead we resort to reciting Psalms in order to ward off evil. A symposium is a kind of recitation of Psalms which lightens one's conscience and even though one remains helpless, one at least enjoys the solace of voicing one's opinion together with others. I will therefore join this symposium-prayer meeting and have my say on the questions proposed.

1. I do not regard Negro anti-Semitism as essentially different from the normal, deeply-rooted Christian anti-Semitism, nor do I believe that it will harm the Negro struggle for equal rights. Negro anti-Semitism becomes a special threat only at times of racial outbreaks when the darkest instincts of a Negro mob break loose. At such times Negro anti-Semitism becomes doubly virulent as it is fed by hatred of both Jews and whites, and the Jew becomes its prime victim.

2. I doubt very much whether Jews as a group respond with a distinctive blacklash to Negro anti-Semitism. We are accustomed to general anti-Semitism, and since we possess no organized backlash to it, we do not react in any unique way to the special gift which Christendom has bestowed upon us in the form of several million black anti-Semites. If Jewish participation in the Negro struggle for equality has been weakened, this is a part of the general reaction in America and of the prevailing fear that has gripped the American people as a whole. Some Negro leaders were delighted that they have succeeded in terrorizing the white population. The white backlash expresses itself not in the behavior of a few thousand white hooligans in the big cities, but in the unspoken fear and in the bewilderment of millions of white Americans at developments in recent years.

3. I am convinced that anti-Semitic sentiments played a prominent role in the recent Negro outburst. Jewish welfare is always the first to suffer when a Christian mob goes on a rampage. This has been so throughout the ages. Jews labor for years, and when Christian mass hooliganism breaks out, they are the first to be plundered. The Negro rioters knew which were Jewish businesses in their neighborhoods (often these were the very same ones that extended credit to them) and "settled" accounts with them when disorder reigned.

4. I am not a statistician but I have the feeling that Jews are heavily represented in the ownership of low-cost housing and small businesses, for the simple reason that they earn their livelihood from small capital investments. A Jew will labor until he saves up a few thousand dollars which he then invests in some small enterprise. Despite the Christian myths

that Jews control international capital, the fact remains that
the biggest banks and large scale industry are Christian-
owned. In their vast majority Jewish businessmen are
engaged in minute enterprises. This is so today, and it was
even more so a short time ago when Jewish immigrants
emerged from the sweatshops and turned to operating
candy stores, groceries and tailor shops.

5. It is not necessary that the Jewish community should
advise Jewish storekeepers to stay away from Negro neighborhoods. The storekeepers will do so themselves. Those who
own businesses in Negro neighborhoods from before, are looking for opportunities to run away from Watts and Harlem.
They know very well that uncurbed Negro anger will hit
them first. This they have now learned. It is a pity that they
had not learned this lesson earlier from Jewish history and
experience.

6. This rhetorical question concerns only the worst form
of assimilation. It is true that there exist Jews who forget
their past and their historical experience and believe that
they can escape their destiny by evasion. But most Jews are
not assimilated socially and culturally to the point of
self-denial. Assimilation takes on many forms, and most of
what we commonly call assimilation is merely a form of
coexistence, the assumption of superficial protective colora-
tion, the fear to appear different.

7. I do not believe that Jews owe a greater debt to the
Negro struggle for freedom than do our Christian neighbors.
For one thing, we are not historically the enslavers of the
Negro; it is rather our Christian neighbors who interpreted
the Bible to find sanction in our time to hating other races
and keeping them in bondage. Personally I never felt the
least prejudice against Negroes, but I never had to invoke
my Jewishness to teach me tolerance. I have lived long
enough to realize that, as a matter of course, Jews always felt
more humanely and decently toward their Negro neighbors
than the Christians. In general, Jews are "vegetarian"
haters; their hatred is superficial and does not feed on
murderously zoological sources.

Therefore I submit that Jews who actively participate in

the Negro freedom movement do so not in the performance
of a specifically Jewish duty but as civilized human beings,
modified by the special Jewish inability to hate passionately.
No, I do not believe that we have any special duties as
Jews. Our duties as human beings apply to all oppressed
people; special duties we owe only to ourselves as Jews. I
could only wish that Negroes felt as little special duty to hate
me as a Jew as I do not feel any special obligation to love
them because I am a Jew. But as a human being and as an
American I cannot rest that millions of my dark-skinned
brothers are treated with such savagery. It is a nightmarish
situation, when one recalls that this is taking place in America
during the last third of the twentieth century.

8. The eighth question does not apply to me. The ninth
question I wish to answer with a categorical negative. The
Negro leaders have not tried to uproot anti-Semitism from
among their people. All their statements in this regard were
lukewarm and *pro forma* only. We are able to judge such
statements and know when they come from the heart. The
Negro leaders have been too busy with their own affairs,
with their Movements, with their ambitions and inter-group
rivalries. Often they were silent though they should have
spoken out in protest when they regarded certain elements
in their ranks as strategically important to them. In the end
they proved badly mistaken, for the advocates of Black
Power are now beyond control and have turned the tables
on those who formerly coddled them.

Negro leaders should feel concerned about the fear felt by
white Americans. The fact that whites are afraid to walk
through Harlem, that white taxi drivers are justifiably fearful
of taking fares to Negro neighborhoods should arouse serious
concern among Negroes. Some Negroes may feel momen-
tarily elated that they have succeeded in frightening the
white population. But integration in housing and in schools
is undermined by this fear.

This fear is an outgrowth of certain methods employed
by the Negro revolution and these should be reconsidered
and revised. White backlash—not that of white hoodlums,
but that stemming from silent terror—is also a consequence

of certain tactics of the Negro struggle which have become outdated. We tend to forget that the struggle is for equality, but that equality cannot be founded on hatred and fear.

10. I have always regarded the Negro "Muslim" groups as more Negro than Muslim. The Arab pedigree of these groups is as dubious as their Mohammedanism. Malcolm X was the outstanding personality of the Muslim movement, but even when he advocated the most extreme tactics in the Negro struggle for freedom he was welcomed, and held in reserve as a weapon, by many non-Muslim Negro leaders.

11. So far as Negro-Jewish consultative bodies are concerned, with all their implied pious assumptions of a common heritage of oppression, minority status and dispersion— these would at best be little more than joint prayer meetings. And what harm is there in a prayer meeting?

The issue that confronts us is that soon it will no longer be a problem of integration but of simple coexistence on human terms. So far as I am concerned, nobody can make a white "backlasher" of me. Many years before the Negro revolution and the Supreme Court ruling on desegregation I protested against the condition of the Negro in America. What should concern us is the growth of "blacklash"—revanchist, destructive, anti-white vandalism, the posture of "perish my soul with the Philistines." I have experienced the entire evolution of the pauperized, bedbug-ridden East Side, extremes of discrimination against Jews and bitter degrading poverty, but it never occurred to us during those dark days to resort to rioting.

B. Z. GOLDBERG

I REMEMBER Harlem before it was "Harlem," the Negro ghetto, sore-spot of the city, epitome of racial indignity and injustice. It was then the symbol of having arrived. The uphill road then led from Ellis Island by way of the lower

East Side to the upper East Side, and finally Harlem; the peaks of West End and Park Avenues were beyond the horizon.

Harlem was then largely Jewish. Though not the symbol of affluence, it was the home of "better class" people who knew how to live. Lenox Avenue was a second class 57th Street, as 125th Street was a superior 14th Street.

On Lenox Avenue one could then meet such notables as the "Monarch of the Yiddish Stage," Jacob P. Adler, walking in royal dignity, cane in hand; and on Sabbath morning, the diminutive Cantor Yossele Rosenblat, in his shiny stovepipe, which balanced his long rounded beard. Sholom Aleichem, too, could be seen on Lenox Avenue— sneaking into a movie house to see a Charlie Chaplin comedy.

This was Harlem at the outbreak of the First World War, which was to change many things, including the character of Harlem.

There was a Negro community in Harlem even then, occupying the North-East corner, from Madison Ave and 133rd Street to the Harlem River. Here the streets were poor, the houses neglected, but not much more so than the poor sections on the East Side inhabited by white people. There seemed to be no animosity in the relationship between the two races. Both races seemed to take each other, and their respective circumstances, for granted. The intelligent colored person certainly resented his lot, but he did not vent his resentment on the white people about him. Both were trapped in a regrettable social situation. The attitude of the Jews in Harlem toward the Negroes was not unlike their attitude to the poor, ignorant *goyim* in their home towns of the Old Country. The color of their skin did not matter; it simply did not register.

One day, back in 1915, I accompanied a Jewish insurance agent on his route in Harlem. He was doing a thriving business selling a life insurance policy at a premium of 30 cents a week, collectible weekly, which paid $200 at death. The amount was small; it was intended to provide, not for dependents, but for a decent funeral. In the absence of family ties, a chief dread among colored people in Harlem at that time seemed to be a pauper's grave. The insurance process was simple: the client merely had to answer a few questions: name, address, age, place of work, married (the answer almost invariably, no), children (answer almost invariably, yes), and then the signature. In case of illiteracy, a cross, witnessed by the agent, sufficed. The policy lapsed as easily—one month's arrears plus two weeks grace.

At one apartment we came upon an exceptionally intelligent woman. Yes, she had been married, though she no longer lived with her husband. A daughter of about fourteen sat in a wooden rocking chair holding a book. She had just been graduated from grammar school. Would she like to go on to high school? The girl did not reply. I turned to her mother: "Why don't you send your daughter to high school?" The woman paused for a moment, and said: "She can wash white folks' floors without a high school education."

Those were bitter words. Yet the woman did not seem to associate the two of us with the lot of her race. Our encounter was cordial, her manner with the insurance agent particularly amiable, as with an old personal friend. She may not have reasoned it out, but her resentment was against the system rather than the people, against the white man's world rather than the white people with whom she had personal contacts.

My first contact with Negroes took place almost sixty years ago in Traverse City, Michigan. There were only three Negro families in town. They enjoyed equal rights, and were treated with due respect. Socially, however, they remained outsiders. The only white people visiting them were Jews, who were also treated as outsiders. My mother could barely speak English, but with the few words she knew she managed to establish a friendship with Mrs. Patterson, generally known as Phoebe, whose backyard bordered on ours. Phoebe, my mother said, was a very nice woman, with a heart of gold; her children were better behaved than the Jewish children.

At the University of Iowa, where I passed my freshman year in 1912, there were three Jewish students and one Negro. The Jewish boys were accepted with a degree of deference. They were favored in all campus activities, but were not invited to house parties. The Negro was only accepted as a fellow-student in classroom and laboratory.

He and I never discussed matters pertaining to Negroes. Once I did touch on this subject, and he looked away. I soon learned that race was not a subject for polite conversation. Even the word Jew was avoided in mixed company, the Gentile referring to Jews as Hebrews, and Jews among themselves referred to *Jews* as Yehudi.

The tides of change that came in the wake of the First World War altered the character of Harlem. The white families were now financially able to seek better quarters in more desirable neighborhoods. Negroes from the South flocked in search of a better life in New York. Negro Harlem expanded in all directions; 125th Street was now a white commercial artery in the heart of a colored community. There was nothing strange about this. There always have been Jewish stores in non-Jewish neighborhoods in all parts of the world. The Jewish merchants of Harlem said that in many ways the new Negro customers were preferable to the earlier white ones.

The nineteen-twenties marked the beginning of social stratification in Harlem, which introduced status consciousness. "Higher class" Negroes wanted to dissociate themselves from Harlem's "lower class"; those who had "arrived" in Harlem began dreaming of the white beyond, while those who failed were consumed by frustration. Even the lowly felt a need of identification, having lost the sense of belonging they had enjoyed in their communities in the South. Two trends developed which had some bearing on the Jewish community. One was a search for identity and self-expression in esoteric religious cults, the other a vision of escape by means of a return to Africa.

One day, at my newspaper desk, I received an invitation to a *bris* (a circumcision) in Harlem, signed Samuel Valentine. The existence of Negro Jews in Harlem was by then generally known, but the Jewish community took little interest in them. Not on account of their color. Had they come as converts to Judaism, they would have been accepted like any other proselytes. But they claimed to be Abyssinian

Jews, or descendants of one of the lost ten tribes in Africa,
which was obviously nonsense. Here was a chance to meet
the Negro Jews in person.

Samuel Valentine was a tall, brown man, soft spoken and
polite. His apartment on 133rd Street was simply furnished
and neat, and on another street could have been the home
of a white worker or small shopkeeper. There were several
Negroes in the house, mostly women, and two white Jews,
one a *mohel* to perform the circumcision, and the other a
busybody who was managing everything. The ceremony was
delayed, because someone had gone out to buy herring at
the Jewish grocery. Why herring? "Were you ever at a *bris*
where they did not serve herring?" the busybody said to me.
After the herring was brought, the ceremony was performed
much as in other Jewish families at that time.

When this little Negro Jewish boy grew old enough to go
to school, he was readily accepted in a Talmud Torah on
116th Street. There he also had his bar mitzvah.

Valentine gave me the background of his Jewishness. He
was born and raised on the island of Jamaica. When still
young his grandmother confided to him that their family
had always been Jewish. After he moved to Harlem, and a
Negro Jewish community was being organized, he readily
joined. The others were just becoming Jews; he had been one
for generations.

Another Jamaican Negro, Marcus Garvey, came to Harlem about the time of the Balfour Declaration, and established a newspaper, *The Negro World*, which preached a
kind of Negro Zionism. He maintained that all Negroes
everywhere were one people, and should regard themselves
as one nation and look to the return to Africa for their
national salvation. He organized an all-Negro corporation,
"The Black Star Steamship Company," to be manned exclusively by Negroes, to ply between the West Indies, the
United States and Africa. He appealed to his followers for
funds and was literally showered with donations. I do not
know whether Marcus Garvey knew about Zionism when he
started out from Jamaica, but when I met him in New York,
at the height of his glory, he kept asking how the Zionists
"operated."

During the depression and the social unrest of the 1930's, the first strains appeared in the relations between the Jews and Harlem Negroes. Inasmuch as these tensions appeared on all social levels, they changed the Negro image of the Jew.

On the lowest level, the so-called slave-market engendered resentment.

As the most marginal people in the city, the Harlem Negroes were the first to feel intensely the economic pinch. The Negro woman has always been the main provider of the Negro family, the husband's contribution, where there was one, has been secondary. Now the men became jobless. And just then the call for houseworkers, almost the sole source of employment for Negro women, took a precipitous drop. The middle-class white women cut their household expenses to aid their hard-pressed husbands. Pay for housework fell to twenty-five cents an hour, and even at this rate work was difficult to find. Negro women congregated at certain corners of the lower-middle-class neighborhoods where they might be picked up for a day's work. The strong women were taken first, the others often felt obliged to accept even lower pay.

These slave markets were located in the poorer Jewish neighborhoods. Many of the women coming to select Negro help had never had their housework done for them—they now first came to the market because of the cheapness of the labor. Poor themselves they had the Negro woman do the heavy work, the easier chores they did themselves, and they were stern taskmasters. Few Negro women realized that their white employer in the market was only a cut or two above their own economic situation. The Jewish woman became the object of their bitter resentment against the low pay and the humiliation of the slave market.

On another level, the Communist propaganda in Harlem laid a basis, however unintentionally, for Negro antagonism toward Jews. Someone at the Negro desk in the Comintern conceived the bright idea of rearranging the United States so as to give the Negroes a few of the states in the South where they would be autonomous, like the national republics in the Soviet Union. The dissimilarity between the two situ-

ations, the fact that the national republics in the Soviet
Union had been national states before being annexed by
the Czars, did not trouble the designers of the Kremlin
Negro policy, who thus anticipated the strange breed of
current Negro opponents of desegregation. This policy called
for the estrangement of the Negro people from their immediate white contacts, and pointed up their exploitation by
whites in Harlem, who happened to be mostly Jewish.

With the Communist propaganda hammering away at
the "white exploiter" and the Nazi propagandists—vociferous in the years preceding the Second World War—identifying the exploiter with "Jew," it was easy for the Harlem
Negro to redirect his natural resentment. Instead of being
against the white *system* he was now against the white
people, especially those of his immediate contacts, and
tended to regard these not as whites who happened to be
Jews, but as Jews—their Jewishness being in some way
connected with their "exploitation" of Negroes. The storekeeper in Harlem was not a simple man who operated his
store long before the Negroes moved into his district, and
who happened to be Jewish, but the Jew come to exploit
the Negro; the rent collector, who happened to be Jewish,
was not regarded as an underpaid employee of a collection
agency engaged by the real owner of the property, which
was most likely a bank, but as a "Jew exploiter."

On a higher level still, well-to-do, educated Negroes who
wanted to move into a white neighborhood and found themselves barred because of their race, blamed "the Jews."
Now, these were intelligent, worldly people who knew better,
and might readily agree that the non-Jews in the white neighborhoods were not only as intolerant, but much more so.
Yet, imitating the white middle class in other respects, the
rising middle-class Negroes also followed their model in
prejudice against Jews.

Thus anti-Semitism came to Harlem. As might have been
expected, the anti-Jewish attitudes evoked anti-Negro sentiment among the Jews involved. Negroes were disappointed
because they had expected more of the Jews; the Jews grew
resentful because of what they regarded as ingratitude for
sympathy shown the Negroes through the years. For all that,

personal relations between Jews and Negroes continued friendly. The propaganda effect was only skin deep. In his heart the Negro knows that the Jew has never regarded him as an inferior human being, or sought to downgrade his personal dignity. The admittedly large participation of Jews in every phase of the struggle for Negro civil rights has reinforced the earlier bonds of amity. The air seemed to clear when a new wave of anti-Semitism flooded Harlem.

This comes from the extreme fringe of the Civil Rights Movement, the frustrated, embittered, confused young Negroes, who scoff at compassion and flout human decency, brandishing the slogan of Black Power, and opposing desegregation. Trading on hate they naturally concentrate on the Jew as the object of their inverted self-hatred. Yet it is easy to overestimate their impact. Their influence is likely to prove both flimsy and short-lived. This annoying phenomenon may be the last before the Negro people emerge on the highroad to full equality and inner freedom.

HARRY GOLDEN

DURING THE question and answer period after a lecture at the Concord Hotel in the Catskills a lady rose to ask: "Mr. Golden, why do you always talk about civil rights? What have the Negroes ever done for us? Don't you know that most of them are anti-Semites?" To which I replied, "As soon as the Negroes have a Concord Hotel I'll stop talking about civil rights. Furthermore, I assure you, a Negro anti-Semite is about as convincing as a Jewish white supremacist."

After all, why should we segregate anti-Semites? Is there really a difference between a colored anti-Semite and a white anti-Semite? Are there different ways of dealing with anti-Semites? And why should we be surprised that there are Negro anti-Semites?

I am convinced, along with Horace Kallen and Maurice Samuel, that anti-Semitism is a *constant* of western culture. Thus as the Negro enters the middle class he will reflect some of the attitudes of his former masters; indeed, as many Jews in the South reflect the attitudes and even the prejudices of the surrounding white Protestant society.

Long before there was any talk of Negro anti-Semitism, Jewish laymen in the South were demanding that their rabbi "stick to religion and leave civil rights alone," precisely the same instructions the Methodist, Presbyterian and Baptist laymen gave their clergy.

I spent a morning interviewing several members of New York's PAT (Parents and Taxpayers). These women were picketing against the bussing of their children to school in other neighborhoods to facilitate integration in the city. After talking to several of these indignant mothers, I finally asked, "Are there any Gentile PAT's?" This was in 1964. In 1966, it is easier to see that the anger of the Jewish PAT is the same anger and fear the Poles of southside Chicago express when they hurl rocks at Negro demonstrators. The only difference is the Poles fly Confederate flags in their forays against the black man.

More, of course, is involved than the fear of property depreciation, sloppy neighborhoods, or interracial marriages. The antipathy to the Negro social revolution involves more, much more: this antipathy is a manifestation of the dilemma of the American middle and near-middle class. Gaining wealth and/or middle-class status is no longer the goal in itself. Instead, these classes are afflicted by the fear of displacement.

At dozens of Jewish fund-raising dinners around the country, I hear whispers on every dais about Negro anti-Semitism. But all I interpret in those whispers is the voice of a man who wants *out* on a commitment.

Negro anti-Semitism takes into consideration, too, the Negro's own resentment. No one who has ever succeeded likes his "first friend." It is much easier to believe one has pulled oneself up by one's own bootstraps.

And the Jew was indeed the Negroes' "first friend" almost from the day the Negro was allowed a friend. The Jew was the first white man to grant the newly liberated Negro some degree of humanity. In the most rigid days of segregation, following the Reconstruction period, Jewish peddlers and merchants began to sell to the Negroes on credit, and a Jew was the first white man to sell the Negro an insurance policy. When most of the uptown stores warned Negroes: "Don't touch unless you buy," the Jewish merchant allowed the Negro to try on the dress or suit or the hat. Elderly Negro women have told me that when the "Jew collector-man" came around they insisted the children see the book with their name written on the account sheet: "Mr. and Mrs. Isaac Jones." Those were the days, in the Southern Christian society, when even the Negro's purchase of a plug of tobacco had to be put on the account sheet of the farmer or landlord for whom he worked.

After the Emancipation, the white native-born Americans kept the Negro securely locked out of the open society. And no other immigrant group paid him the slightest attention: not the Germans, nor the Irish, nor the Poles, nor the Italians, nor the Hungarians, nor the Slovaks; only the Jew established a line of communication, albeit a line of communication in trade and credit merchandising. True, the Jew had an advantage. To him the American Negro was no different from the Gentile peasants among whom he lived and with whom he dealt in the towns and villages of Russia, Galicia, Hungary and Poland.

The Negroes burned the Jewish stores in Watts in 1965 and Jewish stores in Detroit twenty years earlier, because, in the main, Jewish stores were the only stores to burn. *The Jew was often the only white man in a Negro ghetto.* He was there because he was willing to take a chance he could make a modest living out of the poverty-stricken slum.

(It was not until the Negro began to receive a regular government check during the New Deal that the white Christian merchants began to beckon to him for the first time.)

There were times when only the Jewish storekeeper would advance the money a Negro mother needed to bail her son out of the police station. In countless instances, the Jewish store was the place to which the Negro came when in trouble,

when a Negro parent needed a lawyer, or advice on other
important matters.

I do not mean that there was no exploitation of the slum
Negro. Indeed there was. The poor always pay more for less
and the Negro is no exception. Dick Gregory, the Negro
comedian, told me his mother was a pious, decent woman,
who thought nothing of asking, "Go down to the store and
get a few bananas." Though she gave him no money, he
came back with the bananas. If the Jewish merchant over-
charged his customers penny after penny, the Negro children
of the slum helped even the score. The whole process of
racial segregation and discrimination is a dehumanizing process, corrupting both the buyer and the seller, the tenant and
the landlord.

There is no doubt there are Negro anti-Semites; and I
know that as Negroes escape the margins of society, there
will probably be many more Negro anti-Semites. And as
Negroes enter the open society, they may find the Jews a
terrible burden. As his "first friend," the Jew must remain
forever linked to the Negro's original status of racial inferiority. Fellowship with the Jew will prove no bargain for the
Negro. The Jew knew him "when." Negro writers refer to the
"white liberals" as "phonies." We know whom these writers
have in mind and it is neither Bishop Pike nor Lillian Smith.
It was hardly a Freudian slip for novelist James Baldwin to
have said, "Georgia has its Negro and Harlem its Jew."

Indeed at its last NAACP convention I observed the
growing resentment against Kivie Kaplan. Mr. Kaplan, an
Orthodox Jew, is the organization's President. Ten years ago
he liquidated a highly profitable business saying: "I feel that
I must march with the Negroes." But for James Baldwin
and thousands like him yet to come, fellowship with a Kivie
Kaplan will add nothing to self-esteem. James Baldwin will
know he has arrived, for example, not when a Kivie Kaplan
buys his books and invites him to his home, but when a
Senator Herman Talmadge buys his books and offers fellowship. This is still a long, long way off, but without it, I am
afraid the Baldwins will never consider their victory complete, no more than middle-class Jews, even into the third
generation, who aspire so desperately to be welcomed by a

Fair Haven Golf Club or even by the Palm Springs Regatta.

But what has really surprised me is that there are so many Jews who still do not understand the mysteries of anti-Semitism. I've heard arguments recently, from responsible sources, that Jews are disproportionately represented in low-cost housing and retail establishments in the Negro ghetto. Ah, if only our fathers shaved their beards we'd become Americans immediately, is what we youngsters heard sixty years ago; or ah, if only more of the Jews were farmers. . . . There are people who still refuse to believe, *es vet gornisht helffen*, that if there were no Jewish "slumlords" or Jewish stores in the ghetto, anti-Semitism would hardly miss a beat.

But I also wonder at Negro writers who have had so much to say about the "Jewish" slumlord. I think of the thousands of Southern Protestants who have built vast fortunes on Negro slum housing. In every city and town the richest man, next to the mill-owner and the Coca Cola distributor, is the man with what are called, "nigger houses." Fortunes have been made and multiplied. The dwellings, which even today cost about $2500 with rare repair and paint bills, usually house four Negro families who pay their rent weekly and return to the owner every year more than his original investment. The Southern ladies call this property, more delicately, "nigs." An elderly grande dame of the United Daughters of the Confederacy, says, "My father was smart—didn't bother with cotton, or get into the jungle of the mill business; he was smart, left us about two hundred 'nigs.' " These "nigs" are one of the reasons the Southerners fight against (a) slum clearance, and (b) including laundry workers and domestics in the one-dollar-minimum-wage legislation of the several states.

I make no apology for Jewish slumlords of Harlem. I do condemn a society that has tolerated for so long the "nigger houses" of Harlem, Dallas, Watts, Charlotte, and of a thousand other cities and towns of America, owned by Protestants, Catholics, Jews, Negroes, and anonymous insurance companies.

Basically, however, Negro anti-Semitism is peripheral to the whole subject, the main issue. Whether some Negroes

are or are not anti-Semites bears not at all on whether all
Negroes enjoy first class citizenship and move about as free
men, and their children are unimpeded and uninhibited by
segregation and discrimination.

The struggle for civil rights, insofar as some whites have
participated, is not a struggle solely for the Negro. In the
late 1940's it was already clear that the Negro civil rights
movement was for all America, perhaps for the Jews most
of all. The Negro has indeed given the Jew a free ride. The
Negro lawyers who have walked in and out of the American
court rooms during these past twenty years have made the
Constitution of the United States a living document. Their
struggle has convinced Americans, and continues to convince
them every day, that the Constitution means just what it
says. Thus we Jews have achieved a great victory, without
even being exposed to the firing line.

BEN HALPERN

A SPECIAL, indignant tone of surprise and resentment
always creeps into discussions of contemporary Negro-
Jewish relations; perhaps more surprise than resentment on
the Jewish side and more resentment than surprise on the
Negro side, but always indignation. It shows in the formulation of the introductory statement and questions for this
symposium: Have the Jews, "because of their historical experience as a persecuted group, a special debt of greater participation in the Negro liberation movement," and have
they "contributed their proper share?" Has the Negro leadership "done its full duty" in combatting Negro anti-Semitism?

What lies behind the emotions implied in these formulas
of mutual recrimination is the assumption that Jews and
Negroes belong together. The quarrel is especially painful
because it is a family quarrel. At least this is the assumption

on the Jewish side, and on the side of many of the Negro
intellectuals and leaders involved in it.

The question is whether making this assumption is a
healthy way to approach the issues. The question is whether
we do not blind ourselves, by seeing only the ways in which
Jews and Negroes belong together, to the equally, if not
more, important fact that there are many significant ways
in which they do not belong together at all; and indeed may
have conflicting interests.

That kind of self-induced blindness is, in any case, no
longer possible, now that the slogan of "Black Power" has
given a name to facts that grew increasingly obvious in the
past few years. The term is, no doubt, a vague one; and it
seems likely to remain vague for a while, since Negro
leaders have apparently decided that they would cause too
much damage to their movement through ideological disputes
and divisions if they tried to define it more specifically
right now. But its fundamental emotional meaning is quite
clear: it means exactly the same as the equally vague term
of "auto-emancipation" with which Jewish nationalism
began in the 1880's. The Negroes want to run their own
show, without always worrying about the susceptibilities of
whites: even—or especially—of white liberals and even—or
especially—those with powerful positions in the civil rights
movement. They want to be militant in their own style: non-
violent only if it gets them results *they* desire, not merely the
approbation of white pacifists; politically involved, mainly
for their *own*, specific, black community ends, not the common interest in building a progressive society.

It is an unpleasant and revealing fact that the slogan of
"Black Power" hit white liberals as a threat to their personal
security in a way that riots in Harlem and Watts never did.
When Negroes burned down the slums they lived in, the
symbolic rejection of the *whole* of white society was so
grim and brutal that anyone should have understood. But
white liberals were so incredibly smug that they thought they
were not included, and those who indulged in their own
modish forms of protest might even dare to identify with the
destruction. When Jewish stores and property were singled
out for burning and looting, in a new version of pogrom,

Jewish liberals did not feel involved. But what did throw a
scare into them was the announcement that Negroes intended
to run their own "revolution." Here they felt menaced where
it hurt them most, in their identity.

I am unable to sympathize with Jewish liberals shut out
by the slogan of "Black Power," whereas I fully understand
the Negroes who adopted the slogan. It is a curious piece of
presumption to expect Negroes to maintain a "revolutionary"
movement in such terms that whites can find their fulfillment
in it. Least of all can one weep for Jews who, finding themselves unable to live in complete, individual, alienated detach-
ment after rejecting the community they were born in, hoped
to lean on the Negro revolution and use this as the concrete, material foundation for an abstract, fictive community
of protest. The solidarity and self-discipline of the Negro community is a serious matter. It is the beginning of self-respect
and responsibility for them, and the essential prerequisite for
anything else that may be done to advance their cause and
welfare.

Let me add in passing that this is not a time when white
contributions to Negro civil rights organizations are necessarily helpful; and this has nothing to do with white
"backlash." Why should white support, given in greater
measure to one rather than another civil rights organization, be an important element in deciding which group wins
out in the competition to lead and control the Negro community? We Jews do not exactly welcome it when Jewish
organizations, by publicity or solicitation or channels of
influence among Gentiles, claim a larger place in Jewish
affairs than we ourselves are ready to grant them. The whole
set-up of Negro civil rights agencies has been built on a
basis of white support, and it is not to be expected that
this will suddenly be altered. To do so abruptly would cause
too much harm to be thought of. But it would be a healthy
thing if the channels of white cooperation in civil rights and
similar causes were reconstructed in such a way that they
clearly served the general interest, leaving Negro organizations free to work out their own power struggle, as far as
possible, uninfluenced by extraneous considerations.

"Black Power," no matter what the intentions of those

who invented the phrase, also means a general sanction for every impulse to reckless, purposeless violence in the Negro community. Gangs of juvenile delinquents who shout political slogans continue to act, nevertheless, as juvenile delinquents. Anti-Semites who are elevated to the rank of black nationalists remain anti-Semites. When we are asked to understand them, it makes no more sense than it did when we were asked to see in a proper revolutionary light the regrettable violence committed by Ukrainian peasants or Russian and Polish workers during pogroms. We could understand them easily enough—for the history of Zionism knows of its own violent excesses—but it is not our business to understand them. As Jews it is our business to resist pogroms, protest against them, and demand that responsible leaders and authorities control them.

The basis for any healthy Negro-Jewish relation, when the area of "Black Power" is touched, is to understand and accept that we are dealing not with a family quarrel, but with the distinct and maybe even conflicting interests of separate groups. It is not only puerile and self-indulgent of Jews to protest against their exclusion from Negro affairs because of the "Black Power" slogan; it would be foolish and self-destructive of the Negroes to take any other course. In the same way it is a pointless evasion for Negroes to try to explain the roots of Negro anti-Semitism to Jews. This problem child is not our child, no matter how liberal we may be, and it is not our business to understand him, but to insist he behaves. Only the illusion that we are all one big family, sharing precisely the same responsibilities, still confuses this issue, to the detriment of all concerned.

This cuts two ways, of course. It is pretty useless to scold Negro leaders for anti-Semitism as if they were our naughty siblings. On a moral plane, we *are* all brethren, but if Negro leaders need only preaching to in order to control Negro anti-Semitism they would have undertaken the job long ago. The task involves a tricky problem in intra-community politics, just as the job of controlling Zionist terrorist organizations did in its time. It is, in the same way, a job the Negro leadership will someday have to accomplish in its own interest, if it does not wish to lose control to irresponsible elements, and with it, the hope of a brighter Negro future. Our moralizing is of little effect here, but the fact that anti-Negro violence in Northern cities is led by groups like Rockwell's American Nazis ought to have a greater impact.

It follows from all I have said that I can place no great hope in Negro-Jewish consultative bodies, if their aim is "to foster greater understanding . . . on the basis of common historical experiences of oppression, dispersion and minority status." Such bodies, devoted to examining not misunderstandings but conflicts of interest between the two groups as they arise, are another, far more serious matter. It is worth devoting a final comment to indicating just how serious it is, what important consequences it entails, if attempted, how grave are the problems it proposes to confront, and how slight a prospect there is of a full and successful attack on them.

The basic Negro-Jewish conflict is the same as the basic Negro-white conflict, in specific application. What the Negro wants is what the white has, and he wants it *now*. The whites who have what Negroes are going to want to take *next* are very often Jews. The stores in Harlem, the teaching jobs and civil service appointments are rungs on the ladder Negroes have to climb over the toes of Jews, just as they have to make Irish and Italians move over in the construction trades. These are the issues likely to be brought before any Jewish-Negro consultative committee that may arise.

If these issues are raised by way of teen-age gangs on the rampage with bricks and torches, we can treat them in no other way than as a kind of pogrom. If they are brought up as a matter of social equity for joint deliberation, we have to meet them on their merits. By this I do not mean a pious mouthing of liberal phrases about freedom and opportunity. That kind of talk belongs in brotherhood meetings where we assume we are all one family. Here we have to deal with interests of groups—conflicting interests, indeed—which can only be settled by direct action, aimed not to illustrate a principle (of formally equal opportunity and reward according to merit) but to achieve a result (the equalization of Negro social and economic status). For this to be achieved *next*, and as nearly as possible *now*, Negroes will have to demand that Jews, among others, make room for them; and Jews will have to consider how this can be done at the least possible cost to Jews. It can certainly never be done without cost.

These are the shape and dimensions of the problem. What it implies is, both on the Negro and the Jewish side, a disciplined, functional community organization. The Negroes can make demands without such an organization, of course; but they can do very little without it to take advantage of whatever responses they may elicit. The Jews could neither carry out any program to make room for Negroes at the expense of Jews nor help find suitable new adjustments for Jews who might be affected with the kind of loose quasi-organization the community now possesses.

Anyone who sets up such joint consultative bodies hoping to deal with real problems had better be prepared for slow and painful and very little succes. What the Negroes want *next* may be hard to obtain *now;* but the process of obtaining it practically, in society and not merely the legislature, through give-and-take with one's neighbor and not by demonstrations alone, could be heartening. As for the Jews, if the will to work out practically at least some of the concrete problems involved in Negro-Jewish relations could compel them to give even a little more substance to their communal organization, it would be a significant gain in itself.

ARTHUR HERTZBERG

THE RELATIONS between Jews and Negroes are deteriorating. There is now the seed of conflict and, perhaps, even of tragedy.

The confrontation between Jews and Negroes is created, in the first place, by some hard sociological facts. In every big city in America the Negro ghetto, from Harlem to Watts, is inhabiting an area which was last occupied by Jews. Many of the white landlords, and, perhaps most of the shopkeepers who remain in such neighborhoods, are left over from the earlier days. In the Negro ghetto the conflict between landlord and tenant, between seller and buyer, between creditor and borrower is, therefore, very often between Negro and Jew. For example, some 750 stores were destroyed in the Watts riot a year ago; it is reliably estimated that five hundred were owned by Jews.

On the average, Jewish landlords and shopkeepers are perhaps kinder to Negroes than the rest; or perhaps there is no difference. There is reason to believe that the roughest treatment meted out to the poorest elements in the black ghettos comes not from white but from Negro shopkeepers and landlords. All this does not matter to the teenager who feels that he must steal a bicycle, because he cannot possibly imagine ever being able to buy one. "I want what you've got," means to him that he wants what the owner of the bicycle store has, and that owner is most often named Greenberg or Cohen.

In the second place, as both James Baldwin and Nathan Glazer have seen, Negroes and Jews require quite different things from American society. The battle of the Jews for their equality in America has been waged under the slogan of a career open freely to talent. Jews did not ask any advantages to repay them for centuries of persecution. The structure of the Jewish family outlasted the ages, and the Jewish tradition of learning remained strong. Sam Levenson has recently exaggerated when he proclaimed that the home of his immigrant parents had "everything except money," but it did provide such moral and intellectual foundations that the Jewish individual needed nothing more than a partially open society to make it possible for him to advance rapidly. For the Negro, the problem is in reverse. Slavery disintegrated the family and subjection permitted very little learning to penetrate. Most Negro individuals in America today need opportunities which are weighted in their favor to give them a fair start.

The conflict between these two outlooks can only become

sharper. With some variations all minorities in America have used the same path of ascent: the governmental bureaucracies and the service occupations. Both fields could be entered by individuals far more easily than the dominant power structure of banks, insurance companies, steel mills and the like. A child of a minority can enter the bureaucracy because his people vote, and he can get into the service occupations because there one is essentially in business for himself. The Negro is now bidding for these places, and the bid must increase as more Negroes attain higher education. It is inevitable that the first Negroes to appear in considerable numbers will not, on the average, place as high on competitive examinations as their white peers, precisely because they will have begun from a disadvantaged starting point. Inevitably, however, they will demand access to the roles in society for which they have prepared themselves, and they will regard any barriers, no matter how seemingly reasonable, as white self-protective devices. As Negroes fight ever harder to enter the higher levels of the bureaucracies, the staffs of hospitals, or the university faculties, they will be encountering a rather large proportion of Jews, who made it out of their ghetto a generation before through these very avenues.

The beginnings of this confrontation are already overt in the literary field. At this very moment Jews supposedly dominate the American literary establishment. Jewish novelists have made their particular *angst* the central theme of creative letters, and Jewish critics are the arbiters of taste and style. There is no Gentile backlash, but angers are being expressed in some of the Negro publications. The "Jewish" establishment that is being attacked has been notably pro-Negro, but this does not matter to the Negro attackers. For that matter, Jewish intellectuals in social work, in the various professions and in the university faculties have been consistently in the lead among those whites who were doing battle for Negro rights. Among the very young, perhaps a majority of the whites who have worked and died with SNCC in the South have been Jews, but that is now being forgotten and even condemned. There is a kind of ruthless logic to "I want what you've got." That which Jews have,

from a bicycle in Mr. Greenberg's store to the seat on the
Supreme Court held by Justice Fortas, is increasingly appearing to Negroes to be that part of what the whites have,
which Negroes can get most easily.

The tragedy that seems to be coming is all the more
somber because both Negroes and Jews are both the puppets
and the victims of ideas which the Christian West announced
and did not mean. Almost the only point at which the
Negro, historically, has been part of the majority is in the fact
that the Negro is a Christian. Despite its recent bad conscience, the Christian West has systematically participated in
the enslavement of the Negro, at the very least, by its
silence. The only Christian "principle" which the Negro has
been able to share unreservedly, and from which he has not
been excluded by white Christians, has been anti-Semitism.
In the act of hating Jews the Negro joins the majority for he,
too, is now using the Jew as scapegoat.

The Jew, too, is in a trap. The Jews never did succeed in
achieving their unquestioned share in the new age of the
liberal revolution. Jews retain very recent memories of their
own battles to enter Western society; they remember the
scars of exclusion. This does not necessarily, at this moment,
lead inevitably to liberal conclusions. There is, therefore, a
kind of ambivalence among Jews: on the one hand, both
religious tradition and historic memories impel us to side
with the Negro; on the other hand, there is the unworthy
impulse to become part of the majority, as white men. In
sum, if the Negroes can "join" society through anti-Semitism,
Jews can "join" it as whites.

Perhaps the saddest element in this whole frightening
picture is in the fact that Jews are the people who are best
able to understand the rhetoric of Black Power, even though
they are most directly on the firing line of its attack. Stokely
Carmichael is really the most radical kind of Negro Zionist.
He talks exactly the language of those Jews who felt most
violently angry at the sight of Hitler and most hurt by the
good people who stood aside.

What Mr. Carmichael is asserting is "Zionist" in more
fundamental respects than the anger that it is expressing.
He is saying very simply that no community is given freedom

or equality as a gift; that not even one's best friends can be the leaders in a struggle in which their personal futures, and those of their children, are not involved except indirectly; and that no community has any real position in this nasty world unless it translates its appeals to conscience into the beginnings of a power base, both economic and political, of its own. But this was precisely what all the Zionist theorists, from Herzl through Borochov, were talking about.

Classic Zionist analysis applies very precisely to the other side of the situation, that of the Jews. In the very midst of the Russian pogroms in 1881 a number of younger Jewish intellectuals recognized a horrible paradox: that the complaints of the peasants of Russia had substance, even though the first targets of the dispossessed were equally miserable Jewish shopkeepers. Both the peasants and the Jews were products and victims of a system of oppression that they had not made; nevertheless, the resentments of the peasants were channelled against Jews because it was Jewish shopkeepers to whom they owed money, directly. Moshe Leib Lilienblum observed that a social revolution was possible in Russia which would do justice to the majority of the people and yet would be hurtful to the Jews. There cannot be a scintilla of doubt that justice for the Negro in America today will cost something, and that an outsize proportion of that cost will have to be paid by Jews.

Having said all this, I can address myself to the specific questions that were raised for the symposium, only by saying that I am out of sympathy with their basic tone and with what seems to me to be their underlying presumptions. The notion that there are "true interests of the movement for Negro civil rights" which anti-Semitism does not really serve is true, but only in the ultimate, moral sense. The true interests of the Negro at this moment are, from his point of view, in going as far and as fast as he possibly can, and he has now realized that the only way to go there is not through gradualism and "popular front" alliances but through making the Negro ghetto too explosive to ignore—and, alas, an all too available way of doing this is to use Jew-hatred. In such a situation there can only be power bargainings between groups and communities. Jews must resist, through all the influence and power at their disposal, and they must engage in the quest for accommodation, at a cost acceptable to them.

In the light of these reflections it seems to me that all of the other questions raised for this discussion fall by the wayside. The Jewish establishments have made more liberal declarations about Negroes than any other, but that makes no difference to a revolutionary situation. The issues between Jews and Negroes are not misunderstandings between the two groups but hard questions about power and position. It is ridiculous to pretend that at this moment in American history, the texture of Jewish and Negro experiences are similar. The Jews are the most vulnerable of the haves, and the Negroes the most unfortunate of the have-nots. They may have some rhetoric in common; they are together the heirs of moral imperatives; but the real question is what love and justice mean, concretely: how many Jewish school principals are commanded by the joint Negro-Jewish commitment to morality, and Jewish memories of persecution, to go sell shoes, so less well-trained Negroes can hold their jobs. This is a problem not for the writers of liberal resolutions. If it is to be solved it must be dealt with by an odd team: Talmudists, who apply moral norms to concrete problems, and power-brokers.

PAUL JACOBS

THE SIX Negro women and I sat, talking, in an apartment in the Nickerson Garden public housing project in the heart of Watts. Outside, the kids were screaming at play and the bells of an ice cream truck kept playing the same tune, maddeningly, over and over again. The women were all friendly, for I had been brought there by someone they trusted.

They were talking about the "Jewboys," about how they

get cheated, especially by one man, whom they always call "Leon the Jewboy." They explained that on the 1st and 15th of each month, "Leon the Jewboy" drives a truck into the housing project, takes out a rack filled with clothes and rolls it from door to door trying to sell them merchandise on credit. "Jewboys" weren't the same as white people to them, and when I asked them how they tell the difference, one woman patiently explained it to me, as if I was a slow-witted but nice child:

"The white man don't have time to be knockin' on no door, and that Jew, that's his stick—(as I heard her use the word "stick," I realized that here is cross-culturalization at its best or worst—a Yiddish word being used in an anti-Jewish context)—he's been doin' it for years, that's why he controls most of the money. Now I know a Jew isn't a white man and besides he talks Jew—"

Another woman interrupted, "He'll tell you, you don't have to pay me but a dollar or whatever you got, you just give it to me and I'll come back—"

"Uh Huh," said the first woman, "the white folks don't do *that*."

"You can pay him two dollars a month and he'll come back for the next twenty years," chimed in still another, as they all broke out laughing.

They vied with each other in telling me stories of how they'd been cheated, and there was even an element of bitter admiration in their description of how the "Jewboys" take advantage of their foolishness and ignorance. I asked if they ever saw any Jews in the project except the salesmen. There was a pause while they thought, and then someone said, rather incredulously, "For what? For what would they come down here? They come down here they're gonna make them some money, you know. The 'Jewboy' always done that. I remember my father used to tell about when he'd go into a store to buy a suit, and he'd put the suit on and the Jew catched it in the back and holds it and says it fits real good. And when you get home two folks can wear that coat."

They burst out laughing again, and continued regaling me and each other with stories of how they've been "taken by the

Jew." They never say "Jewish," either, but always refer to
"the Jew" or the "Jewboy." I asked whether any of the white
storekeepers in the area cheat, too.

"They all cheat," is the answer I got. "They have to cheat
'cause we don't have nowhere else to go. If I know you don't
have nowhere else to go, I'll charge you what I want because
you ain't got no other way to go and no transportation to
go and get it. So you want it, you need it, so I'll make you
pay for it. You know you're gonna buy it."

These were poor Negroes speaking, all of them either
welfare recipients or women working at very low-paid jobs,
and I have heard such discussions fairly often during the
past year. In the area of Los Angeles where they live, no
adequate transportation system exists, so there is no place
for them to do their shopping except at the fringes of the
housing project. And before August, 1965 when the burning
and rioting took place, most of the furniture and clothing, and
a good many of the liquor and grocery stores in the area
were Jewish-owned, and many of the owners did act in the
way described by the women. Specifically, in addition to
charging high prices for often inferior merchandise or stand-
ard brands, some shopkeepers also made the women purchase an item like a broom or a mop before they would
cash their welfare checks. The liquor store owners, too, often
insist that a bottle of expensive liquor be purchased before
they will cash the checks.

It is difficult to estimate just how widespread among
Negroes is the view of the Jew as the cheating merchant.
The poor Negro's perception of a Jewish world is a very
limited one; he knows little or nothing of Jewish culture,
religion, or of the Jewish intellectual. No Jewish organizations function among the poor Negroes of Los Angeles.
And since even middle-class or wealthy Negroes are hardly
ever more than a generation removed from being either poor
themselves or the children of poor Negroes, the Jew as seen
by the poor remains a distinct impression, even among those
who have escaped poverty.

It is difficult, too, to find Negro families with more than
one generation's background of education. The percentage
of Negro college graduates whose parents were also college

graduates is still small; the percentage of Negro high school
graduates whose parents also graduated is much smaller
than that of the white population, too.

When I talk with poor Negroes, it never occurs to them
that I am Jewish, and when I tell them that I am, they refuse to
believe it. Since they have little or no connection with the
civil rights movement, they know nothing of the Jewish role
in it, and the names of Mickey Schwerner or Andrew Good-
man are only vaguely familiar to them. When I identify
them and explain that they were two Jewish boys killed by
white men in the south, they find it hard to accept.

However, the notion of the money-grubbing, cheating Jew
is by no means restricted to poor Negroes. A friend of mine,
well-educated, who works for a state agency, has written a
personnel questionnaire satirizing those given by large corporations to Negro applicants for employment. Among the
questions he invented was, "A new Jewish clothing store
opens in the area and claims to give easy credit. It turns out
that the easy credit is 65 percent interest per month. How
long will he stay in business?" His selection of answers
includes: "a) Until he gets rich. b) Until he dies. c) Until
he retires. d) Until the next riot."

But educated Negroes whose contact with the white society
is through involvement with civil rights or improvement
organizations obviously tend to reflect the attitudes most
acceptable in such groups: very little anti-Jewish sentiment
is expressed, and most members of this group seem to understand the important role played by some Jews in the civil
rights movement. But other middle-class Negroes, aspiring to
take part in the free enterprise system by becoming merchants
themselves, see the Jew as a competitor who will try to under-
sell the Negro merchant in order to maintain a hold over the
Negro market.

So the view of "Goldberg" riding around in his "Jew
canoe," as a Cadillac is called by some Negroes in Los
Angeles, milking the community of its money, does have
some credence among Negroes, especially since that view is
encouraged by a few of the fanatical Black Nationalist leaders. But among educated and even intellectual Negroes, this
view of "Goldberg" is modified by reality. They know better,

but their knowledge brings with it no impelling reason to proselytize about the evils of anti-Semitism among the poorer and less educated Negroes. The more cynical among them will joke about the Jewish girls who come to the ghetto; they're glad, they say, to help those girls rid themselves of their guilt.

And, despite the differentiation the women in the housing project make between Jews and white people, there is an obvious overlap in attitude toward both groups. The generalized hostility toward the whole white world takes in the Jews, too, and the specific hostility toward the Jewish merchants contributes to the generalized hate of the white world.

It is very difficult to assess how much hostility is directed toward the Jew, as being separate from the whites: my own estimate, based on only the evidence I have seen, is that the Jews are *not* the primary target of the Negroes' frustration. Instead the order of hate runs, I think, roughly about as follows: white people, police, merchants, and the Jews, as a separate group, last.

Yet the separation made between Jews and white people is disturbing. One reason usually attributed for Negro anti-Semitism is that since the Jews are the whites with whom the Negroes have the most contact, they are therefore venting their animosity toward whites on the handiest target which happens to be Jews. In this explanation, the fact that Jews owned 80 percent of the burned and looted furniture stores; 60 percent of the food markets and 54 percent of the liquor stores may be taken to reflect only that a high percentage of the retail trade among Negroes was conducted by Jews, some of them cheating and unscrupulous people.

But I suspect that the distinction made between Jews and whites may have an additional basis: Negroes deal with a white world of a welfare system, the police department, the schools, the probation officers, the county hospital, the unemployment insurance office, a work situation. Perhaps the notion of the Jew as being different from the white is absorbed from daily contact with this world, and reflects the view held by the society-at-large toward the Jew. Is it possible that the place of the Jew in America is mirrored more accurately in what the Negro perceives as the "white" notion of the Jew?

Yet I want to emphasize that I have never heard of anti-Jewish sentiment expressed by Negroes about any other question than the economic one. The picture of the Jew as the Communist or beatnik seems not to exist among the Negroes; neither is the Jew regarded as an object of religious suspicion or hate, as was true in Europe. The Black Muslims, too, do not overtly preach anti-Semitism, and I have never become aware of any special degree of covert anti-Semitism among them.

What does all this add up to? Unfortunately, not a very encouraging picture, although I do not believe Negro anti-Semitism is a very serious problem at present. In the California Negro ghettoes with which I am now more familiar than the eastern ones, some Negroes do identify the Jew as the exploiting, cheating merchant who derives his income from ghetto dwellers, and takes it all out with him to his fancy home someplace else. Among this group there is very little perception of the Jew in any other role than that of the businessman. At the same time, a kind of bitter admiration exists, directed toward the way in which the Jews allegedly stick together, take care of their own and wield effective political power. No significant forces exist within the ghettoes combatting that view of the Jew, and I see little possibility of any developing. None of the Jewish organizations concerned with anti-Semitism have any impact in the ghettoes.

In the Negro neighborhoods of Los Angeles I know best, "pushing peanuts up Goldberg's nose"—the kids' term for teasing the Jewish store-owner—was a favorite occupation of unemployed teenagers before the fires were set and the stores emptied. But most of the burned-out Jewish stores are still empty, and now the poor Negroes are being exploited by the Chinese. If that process continues, perhaps some day I will hear the kids on the street shouting a phrase that means they're going down the corner to taunt the Chinese storekeeper.

But now I get a terrible feeling of depression of *déjà vu* as

I listen and argue. I have been here before, and heard these same comments all my life. I remember in the 'thirties hearing a North Dakota farmer, the militant head of a farmers' organization fighting mortgage foreclosures, inveigh against the "Jew bankers who were screwing the farmers." When I was a union organizer, I heard workers shout at people going through a picket line, "Don't go to work in a Jewshop! Don't go to work in a Jewshop!" And I have heard union officials, too, talk about the "Jewshop owners" and their smart "Jewboy lawyers."

I have heard the answers given by the Jewish store owners and employers before, too. "The *schwartzers* steal me blind so I'm gonna charge them more." "The colored people don't make their payments, so we have to have a high rate of interest in order to make up for our losses." "In a way, I'm doing the niggers a favor selling to them. No one else will go down there and if I didn't they wouldn't have anything." And the final answer: "Business is business."

If I seem depressed in what I write, and offer little hope for change, this reflects accurately, how I feel. As long as some Jewish businessmen exploit poor Negroes, they will help reinforce some Negroes' distorted and generalized view of the Jew, which is just as inaccurate as the distorted and generalized view of the Negro held by some Jews. But why should a Jewish businessman behave differently than a Christian one or one who worships Buddha? We Jews keep insisting we're no different from anyone else, don't we?

HORACE M. KALLEN

AS I reflect upon *Midstream's* eleven questions about Negro-Jewish relations in America, I find I can answer them more simply and openly as they are put than by weaving whatever answers I come to into a reasoned, logically constructed essay.

So here goes:

1. I cannot see that the anti-Semitism at this time conspicuous among Negroes carries a greater threat to "Jewish well-being" than anti-Semitism among non-Negroes. I believe the sentiment to express a chronic but unconscious propensity which has come to conscious utterance as one of the sequels of the Supreme Court's decision of 1954. This decision was followed by the succession of events which has since signalized the American Negroes' struggle for equal liberty; overt anti-Semitism is an item in the succession; I doubt very much that it can divert Negro Americans from the "true interests" of their struggle.

2. The most signal instance of "the Jewish backlash" I can think of is the vigorous resignation of the executive director of the American Jewish Congress from the National Advisory Board of CORE, which included the statement: "I need hardly tell you that my resignation does not mean that I will in any way lessen my efforts in the struggle against racism to which I have devoted a good part of the last twenty years." It goes with the broader "white backlash" which the diminishing moral contributions of white liberals toward the work of Negro rights groups and the anti-Negro white mobs in Northern cities are held to express. But both Jewish and non-Jewish withdrawals of support and recourse to aggression voice reaction against the manifestation among their Negro fellows of an irrational blind prejudice implying a racist dogma very hurtful to true Negro interests.

The addition of anti-Semitism to the dogma heightens the shock and surprise of the Jews. Although for some time to come developments among Negroes are very likely to increase and diversify the withdrawal of white co-operation, I have little ground for believing that this "backlash" is likely to be anything more than a passing episode such as the history of the struggle for equal liberty at home and abroad is full of. I am inclined to believe that, on the whole and in the long run, Negroes will seek ever more teamwork with Jewish, no less than with non-Jewish white Americans, and that the already quite visible Jewish share will become more so.

3. So far as I am aware, rioting and destruction in the Negro ghettos did not start as anti-Jewish. They were not

motivated like the anti-Semitic pogroms of Slavic Europe, or Hitlerism, or the Ku Klux Klan murders and burnings of Negroes. Anti-Semitism seems to me to have come as an afterthought, an excuse and rationalization for satisfying long-starved needs and lusts in lawless ways. It was of no importance *whose* property was looted or wrecked. That more or less of it may have been owned by Jews is not a primary consideration.

4. As I am not able to judge whether Jews are "disproportionately represented" in the various agencies set up to defend and advance equal rights for Negroes, so I am unable to judge whether Jews are "disproportionately represented" among owners of cheap housing and retail shops in the Negro localities. Concerning the *how* of housing, concerning the business of selling goods and services, I do not believe that any significant differences can be found among Negroes, Jews and non-Jewish whites. In some localities numbers may make Jews more visible, but not worse, and perhaps better, landlords and shopkeepers than their Negro or non-Jewish white competitors.

5. From what I have just said it follows that, if Jewish leaders are to counsel other Jews at all about setting up businesses in Negro localities, they would do wisely, *first*: to call attention to the risks really involved in all enterprises there, and *second*: to advise how those who choose to take the risks might offer a better deal in goods and services than their competitors, and offer it *as Jews*. Such counsel can be construed as a policy in public relations.

6. The Jews of our country, like the other groups which compose our pluralistic and liberty-seeking society, form a variety of diverse and diversifying associations. Each has its own notion of what is correctly, and what incorrectly, Jewish. The anti-Semitism of "white Christian civilization" may be the pervasive pressure which keeps segregation of Jews from one another from becoming complete alienation. It impels many to pursue ways of liquidating their Jewish identity, as many Negroes seek to liquidate their Negroness. For obvious reasons, more Jews than Negroes succeed at this. Each such association adopts a "Jones" of its own to keep up with and surpass.

7. Not every Jewish group that commits itself to a Jewish "Jones" to keep up with is aware of the role of anti-Semitism in Jewish history; or being aware, feels called upon to invoke it as a sanction for the group's commitment to all men's right to be different, and to their equal rights, as different, to life, liberty and the pursuit of happiness. Some do feel so called upon. Others deny that their "Jewish ethics" makes this demand upon them any more than upon non-Jews.

8. This question impresses me as invidious. How is a "proper share" to be defined? How is it to be allotted among "the ramifications" of the rabbinate? We know what commitments the lay Jewish organizations, separately and together (through NCRAC), have made and what actions they have engaged in. But who is to measure their joint and several portions of the "proper share?" And in what terms? By counting heads, broken and unbroken? Dollars? Words? By Negro expectations, and by choosing one of the rival Negro groups as the most reliable voice of these expectations? The Negroes have their church groups, their student groups, their at least two denominations of Black Muslims, their Black Nationalists, Black Power postulants, NAACP, NUL, CORE, SCLC, NCN; there are the Negro trade unions, the Negro fraternal orders, the independent Negro women's organizations. All—and these by no means exhaust the list— purport to speak for all our Negro fellow Americans. Whom shall the rabbinate heed? By what measure weigh their share toward advancing "Negro liberation?"

9. This question assumes that there *is* a duty to counteract anti-Jewish sentiments among "the Negro masses," and that the Negro leaders recognize it as such. It seems to me a piece of wishful thinking. Even if what the question assumes were a fact, "full duty" must signify one thing in terms of Jewish expectations, if any, and another in terms of a Negro leader's sense of obligation. Both would depend for definition on who is accepted as the reliable spokesman for the Jews, and the reliable spokesman for the Negroes. Each may hold the other's measure to be too great or too little. That they would agree on how much is enough, not to say "full," is not a good bet.

10. I do not believe that, on the whole and in the long

run, any aspect of Negro-Jewish relations in the United States is likely to be unfavorably affected by Black Muslim anti-Israel Arabism. It could be offset by the friendly relations between African Negro Mohammedans and Israel. But I can't see that either is likely to make any practical difference in the over-all relations here at home. Black Muslim anti-Semitism is incidental to the cult's rejection of the works and ways of "whitey's" pretensions in religion; it is not a primary motive in this Negro religio-racist defense against "whitey's" Christian racism.

11. Setting up "special Negro-Jewish consultative bodies to examine misunderstandings and to foster greater understanding" between Negroes and Jews seems to me a good thing to do for its own sake. It needs no other sanctions. Keeping such bodies going would depend on their future consequences, not on dubious similarities postulated from past "experiences of oppression, dispersion and minority status." Identifications in this mode are apt at best to be selective and *ex parte*; they could invite the counter that vis-à-vis Negroes, history identifies Jews more readily with the oppressive, dispersing white majority whose victims Jews also are. I think it unlikely that such a would-be appeal to history can make much present sense respecting Negro-Jewish confrontations today and tomorrow. It is the latter that concerns the American Negro; his aims are: Freedom *now;* Equality *now;* Power *now.* The rivalries between Negro groups are rivalries over proposed ways and means to these ends. Each group affirms that its proposals of principle and practice alone can be relied on for future success; each attacks those of its rivals as merely inviting defeat. Altogether, the rival groups count but a small portion of the entire American Negro people, and each competes with the others to engage the allegiance of the ever unengaged multitude of them, who now are more aware than ever before of their sense of white injustice, deprivation, and oppression, and are craving only equal opportunity to live out their lives in equal liberty and equal security, to earn their bread in freedom and to eat it in peace.

Now this majority has been, and will continue to be, Christian. And anti-Semitism is, as the latest researches have again verified,[1] Christian sentiment attached to the New Testament image of the Jew as the villain of the Christian drama of salvation. The sentiment may be contradicted or reinforced by actual contact with Jews as Jews. But the image which sustains the sentiment is independent of contact. It is an article of faith communicated and preserved by Christian teaching. Although it becomes unconscious, it shapes the responses of ex-Christian agnostics, humanists and infidels to the word *Jew* whenever they see or hear it. Where Negro opportunists such as figure in municipal or national politics have, in their ploys for self and power, recourse to anti-Semitism, they exploit this sentiment. When Negro ideologists or cultists such as head CORE, Black Nationalists, or denominations of Black Muslims, have recourse to anti-Semitism, they exploit this sentiment. And so, likewise, do the Negro clergy, who may be considered most responsible among the spokesmen and leaders of our Negro fellow-Americans, and nearest to the mass of them.

For the most part segregated from the white clergy in all denominations of Christian America, the Negro clergy, like the Negro trade-unionists, have come together in organizations of their own to maintain and advance the equal rights of Negroes as Christians as well as citizens. It terms of the faiths they profess and teach, Jews might in fact be black or brown or otherwise "colored": nevertheless as Jews they would be members of a God-chosen people whom God rejects because they reject the divine Savior whom God sent among them to redeem all mankind. Their role in Christian civilization is but a just punishment for this rejection. Now Jews are preponderantly *white;* the evil implied by their *whiteness* is multiplied by the association of exploitation which the identification *Jew* calls forth, without the Negro who feels this sentiment being aware of the *why* or *how* of it.

It seems to me that this unconscious condition is the most pervasive factor in Negro anti-Semitism, and the one that

---

[1] See *Christian Beliefs and Anti-Semitism* by Charles Y. Glock and Rodney Stark, New York, Harper and Row, 1966. The authors are members of The Survey Research Center of The University of California at Berkeley.

merits first consideration by any joint consultative body. Liberation from it must depend largely on steps taken by the authentic representatives of Negro Christianity in this land. There is a precedent in the reluctant Schema on the Jews recently adopted by the Vatican Council. That professions are not enough, goes without saying. Professions of faith, to become meaningful, must be made good in practice. A Negro-Jewish consultative council, having called forth the Negro profession, could well serve to design a reasonable program of co-operation that should strengthen and diversify the already considerable role of American Jews in helping their Negro fellow-Americans to the equal liberty and equal rights as Negro Americans which true Americanism requires and which the Federal Constitution guarantees.

C. ERIC LINCOLN

LET ME say at the outset that I do not accept as "an incontrovertible fact" the suggestion that "there exists a pronounced anti-Jewish sentiment among Negro masses in this country." Let me say also, that to speak of "Negro masses" is to confuse the issue beyond recognition. As I shall illustrate presently, there is in the minds of the *black masses* a sharp distinction between themselves and the traditional "Negroes"—a term now largely reserved for the Negro middle class in general, and the middle-class advocates of integration in particular. Nor is it merely a matter of nomenclature. Two divergent social and political philosophies are involved. Two opposing sets of values are the forces of motivation. We may dismiss out of hand any notion that the Negro middle class is anti-Jewish. Demonstrably, they are not. But I do not think the Negro middle class is being indicted here. What I think is meant are the black masses, the ex-Negro proletariat who now conceive themselves to be "black people."

I know something about the black masses, for like most middle-class Negroes I am a product of that much maligned, seldom understood class of people. The System rewards with a pale patina of respectability those who make it up from the stygian darkness of the black nether-culture, enabling them thereby to shed in part the terrible anonymity of blackness and to take on a quasi-acceptability. Thus do we become "leaders"—called upon to speak for those "masses," who through all their screaming and shouting are not communicating. I do not think the shouting and the screaming has an anti-Semitic tone—at least not yet. But I think it *could* have, and the probabilities are that it *will* have, unless, unless.

A large part of the general problem of racial adjustment here in America derives precisely from the fact that nobody has been listening much of the time to what the black masses have been saying. When we have been listening at all, we have been listening to the better articulated urgings of the Negro middle class and its professional leadership. This is not surprising, for we like orderly and well-articulated representations. This is the way we do business—by lobby and persuasion. The best-heeled lobby with the most attractive portfolio and the most persuasive PR man to sell it gets consideration. We have neither time nor patience for the needs and interests of the rabble, for the rabble have no voice. *At least they have no voice that we have been trained to hear!*

There is a lesson to be learned in remembering that even the traditional middle-class civil rights organizations and their leaders got scant considerations in the old days, even though they were reasonably articulate and acceptably represented. The problem was that there was scarcely any market for what they were trying to sell. There were no pressures for change which white America felt compelled to recognize, and this included the oft-remarked pressures of conscience. Instead, we developed to a fine point the art of racial obliviousness as a sort of national policy which per-

mitted us to respond to the black protest by listening-politely-
without-hearing-at-all—a crocodilish technique so fiendishly
successful in extending indefinitely the status quo. The inevitable result was that the "respectable'" civil rights organizations were forced into the streets in a role that was contrary
to their traditions and to their preferences, and which has
no doubt altered for generations to come the quality *and
the prognosis* for race relations in this country.

What, you will ask, has all this to do with the existence of
black anti-Semitism, or the allegations of it? After all, did
not the Jew go into the streets with the Negro in search of
the Negro's civil rights? Yes, and more than that: Jewish
money, research, planning and legal talent were all instru-
mental in increasing the momentum and the effectiveness of
the struggle. The Jew, whose history of oppression is longer
than that of any other surviving civilization, and whose history is garishly catalogued with the most vulgar atrocities
his haters could devise from one age to another, knows
instinctively that it is but a half-step from racial oppression
to religious or cultural oppressions. The best society—the
safest society—is one in which *all* men are free. This is not to
suggest that the Jewish concern for the black man's
plight has been only enlightened self-interest rather than
moral commitment. In championing the cause of Negro freedom, the Jew in America ran a very serious risk of com-
promising his own. At a time when white anti-Semitism
has been in dramatic (if uneasy) abeyance, it could as
logically have been the strategy of Jewish leadership to adopt
a hands off, don't-rock-the-boat policy toward the civil
rights struggle.

It is understandable then that there is Jewish concern
and resentment over what is perceived as a developing black
anti-Semitism among the Negro masses, but the concern and
the resentment may be unjustified—or at least premature.
What is happening to the black *lumpen proletariat* is not
necessarily, or even essentially, an expression of anti-
Semitism. It is first of all an expression of the developing
sense of identity, which is slowly but certainly energizing
the black masses toward a new chauvinism of undetermined
consequences. In the recognition of himself as a "black

man," an identity which derives its meaning solely as a counter reference to the "white man," who is now conceived, not as the personification of a construct of ideal values, but as the personification of evil, the white man is the eternal antagonist. He is the enemy. Curiously, a "black" identity has always been available to the Negro and without its present overtones of negativism. Except for the enormous social, political and economic limitations with which white America taxed the existential circumstances of being black in white America, it may well have been a logical option. The historic option to live peacefully together as white people and black people in mutual respect has been grievously dissipated, for now it appears that the black masses, for want of other acceptable options, have chosen to be black people as the antithesis of being white. One thing is certain: they do not want to be "Negroes" any longer, for that term—indeed, that *status*—has for them unpleasant and undignified associations. And they have been denied the privilege of being simply "Americans" in the unqualified sense that white nationals are Americans.

Now, to be a "black man," or to be "black people" carries with it in most instances, an emotional concomitant of belligerence and hostility, which is in part a defensive reaction deriving from the insecurity of a new identity, and in part from resentment of continuing abuse. Space does not here permit me an extended treatment of the complex factors involved in the transition from one identity to another, but it is essential to understand that a transition has been made, or is being attempted.

This means first of all, that the docile, subservient, stereotyped Negro with the big laugh and the quaint remark is no longer in vogue. In the neighborhood grocery stores and dry goods shops, and on the "Avenues" where the liquor stores and pawn shops are which provide points of contact for the Jewish merchant and the Negro lower classes, the absence of the stereotype, or his passing, is noted and is interpreted as anti-Semitism. The clown does not clown anymore. The "characters" have changed character. The pleasant and cordial relationship between the seller and the sold takes on a new formality of language, style and ges-

ture. This is not anti-Semitism. This is a new conception of
role and identity.

I have said that the new identity the black proletariat is
struggling to assume may carry with it emotional concomitants expressed as belligerence and hostility. True, but this
hostility when it is directed toward the Jew at all, *is not
directed toward him as a Semite.* It is essentially an *anti-
white syndrome,* and it is anti-white because the white man,
not the Jew, is identified as the perennial oppressor. The
disenchantment of the lower class with the good intentions
or the moral capability of the white rulers is very pronounced
indeed, and it is only insofar as the individual Jew closely
identifies with, or is thought to identify with, the white Christian in his role as a racist does the counter-racism of the
black masses include the Jew. Indeed, the Jew is at this time
far less subject to the black wrath than is the middle-class
Negro, who is suspected of an over-identification—real or
imagined—with the same white man who exploits the black
masses.

A problem does *potentially* exist. The Jew is, after all,
"white," but because of his own long history of suffering,
he has escaped a mass identification of being *the* white man.
He is not thought of as "European," but "Asiatic," which in
the minds of the uncritical is very close to being African.
At the very least a presumption is raised as to whether he is
"white." Indeed, in the Negro folklore, the Jew is very frequently pictured as being a kind of "cousin" to the Negro.
They have an historic bond in that they are both "biblical
peoples." Again, in the folk tales and jokes of the black
masses the Jew is invariably positioned *between* the white
man and the Negro whenever these three "classes" are discussed. A thousand jokes begin with: "Once the white man,
the Jew and the Negro. . . ." Or, "Once Mr. Charlie, Mr.
Goldberg and John Henry. . . ." Inevitably it is the white
man who goes down to defeat, or who is outsmarted in these
wish-stories. Almost never does this happen to the Jew, for
he is usually given a neutral role, or he secretly uses his various aptitudes to help the Negro out-fox the white man.

The problem I mentioned comes alive in the continuing
intensification of racial consciousness and racial identifica-

tion. The Jew will inevitably be asked to declare himself in a way he has not hitherto felt called upon to consider. The black man is acutely aware of the fact that although the Jews have identified themselves with the civil rights struggle, they have not identified themselves with Negroes. There are no more Jews living in the Negro neighborhoods from whence they so frequently derive their wealth than there are white Gentiles. And the typical Jew is just as loath to have a Negro neighbor in his all-white neighborhood as is "the white man." Despite the black man's appreciation of the Jew as a kindred soul linked to him in an historic religious tradition thousands of years old, and in the continuing persecution of a ubiquitous white supremacy, however tragic the choice, the Jew will no longer have it both ways. And again I must emphasize that the still delitescent but clearly indicated attitudes toward the Jew are not substantially different from those now evolving toward the Negro middle class. It will not be a matter of difference, but merely a matter of degree.

A scant five years ago I offered in *The Black Muslims in America* the gratuitous suggestion that we could either do away with racism or expect from the ashes of the Black Muslims another more formidable specter to rise up and challenge our customary way of doing business with the black masses. That specter is here—and the Black Muslims aren't even dead! It is here—partially as a legacy from Malcolm X, in the form of a deepening commitment to *blackness* versus *whiteness* (with the unhappy implications of these oppositional categories). The rallying cry of the black masses is "Black Power," whether shouted in the streets by a handful of "militants," or vibrating in the secret recesses of how many millions of souls grown weary with waiting for the fulfillment of the promise.

However inconceivable it may be to bewildered whites, astonished Jews, and Negroes who publicly disagree: the black masses could not be *less* concerned about "integration." Their present commitment is to values *other* than integration. Any observer who can put off the glasses of what he'd want if *he* were black can see for himself. What *they* want may very well be something other than what they ought to want and they themselves may not be unanimous on goals or strategies. But the rest of us, who claim a more developed sophistication, and who have lived with centuries of white chauvinism, still cannot conceive of a black chauvinism, nor understand the attitudes that motivate it.

There is an argument that the Jewish merchant in the black ghetto should be spared the wrath of rioting blacks because he accounts for but "a minute share of Negro economic misery." This argument is at best unfortunate. The fundamental question is, does the Jewish merchant sell the blacks rotten meat, or doesn't he? Does he overcharge them, refuse to hire them, constitute a drain on the community wealth and welfare, or doesn't he? If he is immune to these practices, it goes without saying that his property should be respected. Even if he is guilty, no right for the destruction of his business is created. But people do remember with a particularly deep resentment those who they feel have sought to take advantage of them. The Boston Tea Party is a memorable case in point. In an emotionally charged situation such as the riot in Watts, nobody sat down to figure out what percentage of the gross exploitation he had suffered came from a particular grocery. But over the years that particular grocery had developed a reputation for short weights and rotten meat, and its "satisfied customers" who never complained openly, never forgot.

It is complained that "a large proportion of the businesses destroyed in Watts and other Negro centers" during the black riots were Jewish-owned. This can only suggest that a disproportion of the businesses there were Jewish, and that the rioters felt a grievance against the owner. The grievance was not because the owners were Jewish, but because they were identified with the continuing exploitation the black masses have come to expect from anyone who is white. The Jew is not *compelled* to be a stranger in the black community. The people would like to see him identify with those forces working for *local* improvement. They would like to see him leave his business and go to bat occasionally on behalf of some of *them* who have had their heads beaten by the police, or their furniture set out on the street. Organized philanthropies are all very well, but they are impersonal, and they do not really say much about the quality of commitment. It is one of the little ironies of our history that practically every church denomination in America has contributed generously to the interests of Negroes in the *abstract,* but when those Negroes as *persons* came to worship in those same churches, they were turned away. And we might add a footnote to history by remarking that much of the Christian philanthropy directed toward Negroes in the abstract was made possible by the miserable exploitation of Negroes in the flesh. One hand giveth, and so frequently, the other hand taketh away.

There is some concern among Jewish leadership that "Muslimism" among the black masses might have contributed to what has been perceived as an increase in black anti-Semitism. I do not think so, or if it has, it is only to the most negligible degree. The emphasis of the Black Muslims and other Islamic cults is not anti-Jewish. It is anti-white and *anti-Christian!* While the Black Muslims feel themselves to be a part of the world-wide body of Islam, there is little room in the Muslim program for the support of anti-Israeli, or anti-Semitic programs or attitudes which have their focus well outside the effective spheres of interest of the black masses. In short, the Negro simply has not learned anti-Semitism yet, so he has no need to develop a rationale for it. It is possible that had he lived, Malcolm X would have developed a more traditional body of Muslim belief and doctrine for his followers, and had he done so, anti-Semitism among the black masses may well have been a by-product.

Some Jews who feel uneasy about the growing estrangement of the black masses, or who perhaps feel vulnerable to anti-white riots in the black ghettos are impatient with Negro leaders for not doing a better job of telling the Jewish story (of philanthropy, civil rights participation and such) to the black dissidents. This is unrealistic for several reasons. In the first place few Negro leaders, if any, believe there exists a significant reservoir of anti-Semitism among either the Negro middle class or the black masses. Secondly, Negro middle-class leadership has not yet been able to sell *itself* to the black masses with any degree of effectiveness. Thirdly, any attempt to sell the Jew to the black masses at this time would be met with suspicion and resentment,

and would surely call attention to a specifically *Jewish* presence in the black ghetto. This could only precipitate anti-
Semitism where there is none, or intensify it if it does exist.

The Jews are under no special obligation to do any more
for Negro freedom than anybody else. Our problem is essentially that of a white majority making up its morals about
whether a black minority can have equal access to the common values of this society. It is not an inter-ethnic problem
at all, except insofar as particular ethnic groups choose, or
are forced to identify with one of the principals. The Judaic
ethic, to be sure, is unequivocal in its demand for a personal
and corporate morality under which the problem could not
exist. But then, so is the Christian ethic, which derives its
principal code from nowhere else but the Jewish religion.

One could argue the expectation that if the Jews are not
especially moved by faith, then they ought to be moved by
experience. Perhaps so. But the best way to forget an
unpleasant experience is not by becoming implicated in
someone else's troubles. To the degree that the Jew has
become involved, he has made a contribution to the Negro's
freedom and to his own. For this, the Negro is, and ought to
be grateful. But the *black man,* that inchoate personification
of the black masses, knows not Joseph. The black man does
not sit in the councils of respectable leadership. He is down
there in the ghetto where the problem is. That is where
the concerned Jew will find him, and that is where the witness
must be made.

WILL MASLOW

THERE ARE precious few Negro-Jewish relations in the
United States today. The middle-class Jew encounters
the slum-dwelling Negro only as a tenant, customer, domestic
servant or employee and rarely does he meet a Negro bus-

inessman, professional or intellectual. (Contact with officials
of Negro organizations are enjoyed only by a handful of
Jewish professionals.) The result is that stereotypes and
myths flourish and rumors take the place of hard facts.

One of these persistent myths is that Negroes hate "Mr.
Goldberg" more than "whitey," that Jewish-owned stores are
a particular target for looters during ghetto riots and that indeed Negro masses are infected with a virulent anti-Semitism.
The facts are, as a national attitude survey taken by the Anti-
Defamation League and soon to be released in book form
reveals, that Negroes are *less* anti-Semitic than white Christians (of the same educational level) and that Negro slum
dwellers overwhelmingly would rather do business with a
Jewish storekeeper than with a non-Jewish one. Jewish-owned
stores were not the target of Negro looters in recent urban
riots; white-owned stores were.

No Negro organization is consciously seeking to incite
anti-Jewish prejudice and national Negro leaders like Martin
Luther King or Roy Wilkins or Bayard Rustin will, whenever the occasion warrants, rebuke anti-Semitic manifestations.

But from time to time ugly anti-Semitic utterances are
heard. How should Jews, and particularly Jewish leaders
and Jewish organizations, react to this conduct? The American Jewish Congress faced this issue several years ago.
The Amsterdam News, an influential Harlem weekly, had
published under screaming front-page headlines a report
that Jews controlled top jobs in New York City's civil service.
We decided that ignoring such material was dangerous and
demanded the repudiation of the phony statistics. *The Amsterdam News* quickly beat a retreat and featured our reply
as prominently as the original story.

The Mount Vernon incident is well known. The educational chairman of the local CORE chapter shouted during
a turbulent school board meeting at which opposition was
expressed by PAT officials to desegregation proposals:
"Hitler made one mistake when he didn't kill enough of you
Jews." I was dissatisfied with the flabby reaction of the
national office of CORE and promptly and publicly resigned
from its national advisory council, a letterhead group. Some

Jews, to my dismay, criticized my action and attempted to equate alleged Jewish hostility to desegregation with the genocidal remark of the CORE official.

Some Jews with a guilty conscience and others afflicted with self-hatred have sought to counter such anti-Semitism by campaigns to improve the business ethics of Jewish landlords and credit merchants. But anti-Semitism, as any student of Jewish history will realize, or indeed any other form of racial or religious bigotry, is not caused by the behavior of the victim. The anti-Semitism that exists among Negroes today is part of the white culture that surrounds them, aggravated perhaps by the fundamentalist orientation of Negro Protestant churches. If all the Jews of Harlem were to move out tomorrow, the image of the Jew as Shylock and Christ-killer would still persist. Anti-Semitism exists in Germany today although there are practically no Jews left in that country. Unable to find live Jews, German anti-Semites display their hatred of Jewry by vandalism in Jewish cemeteries.

The danger is that some Jews will seize upon such anti-Semitic incidents as a pretext against participation in the historic struggle for racial equality in the United States or seek to persuade or pressure Jewish organizations to retreat on this issue. But our answer must always be that our fight for equality is not intended as an act of philanthropy nor one for which we expect gratitude. It derives from our historical experience as a persecuted group and from a sensitive awareness that in the long run racism is a menace to Jewish security.

The fight for full equality in a free society is a Jewish fight because Jews can never be secure in a society one tenth of whose population is condemned to slums, a society ravaged by racism. The same Chicago hoodlums who, proudly wearing the swastika as an anti-Negro symbol, raided Negro neighborhoods, can almost as easily be led into similar raids in Jewish neighborhoods. It is the task of Jewish leadership to teach these lessons to its followers.

But this awareness cannot blind us to the growing black racism in the Negro community, nor compel us to be silent when programs are launched that will split the Civil Rights Movement, undermine the fight for equality and exalt violence as a means of achieving social justice. When Negro extremists demand a Negro principal for a Harlem school, they are undoing twenty years of struggle against Jim Crow Negro school systems. When, in addition, they threaten the physical security of the white principal, they threaten the fundamental basis of our society. Jews, like all other Americans, must resist these trends while continuing their efforts to struggle for full equality in a free society.

FLOYD B. McKISSICK

WHILE IT is true that there exist in Negro urban communities some anti-Semitic sentiments, these feelings and attitudes are given exaggerated attention by members of the majority society and particularly by some members of the Jewish community.

It so happens that Jews are disproportionately represented in the ownership of low-cost housing and in the ownership of retail establishments within the Negro ghettos of many of our large cities. This places Jews in constant contact with the most deprived class of Black Americans who are exploited by a small number of these Jews. Hence, they become the "whipping boy," as it were, for this community. Unhappy confrontations with whites anywhere are ofttimes equated with confrontation with Jews regardless of what group of whites had been involved. The wide spectrum of racial discrimination and oppression has generated resentments that find expression wherever people of the conflicting racial groups encounter each other on any basis of unequal status.

As far as the Jewish backlash is concerned, reaction occurs whenever any Negro makes an anti-Semitic or derogatory remark and this has been used to withhold or, at least, to limit contributions to civil rights causes. Great sensitivity exists in this respect, partly a psychological reaction to the

recent genocidal experience under Hitler and partly because
of the dislike of Jews to receive criticism of a special ethnic
nature. Jews do identify themselves culturally and socially
with white American society, but at the same time seldom
lose the realization that historically they have also been victims of white Christian oppression.

The Rabbinate has not contributed a great deal to the
Negro freedom movement. It has given philosophical and
financial support, but has developed few programs to aid the
quest for equality of Black America. Young Jews, however,
have participated in large numbers in the Southern Freedom Movement and still participate in Northern protest
movements.

It is deplorable that some writers attempt to give Jews a
status of responsibility exceeding that of other white Americans toward the development of the Civil Rights Movement.
It is true that historically they have faced oppression and
persecution but, as Americans, their responsibilities are the
responsibilities of all Americans.

Many parallels exist between the history of American
Negroes and that of the Jewish community. The stress
upon cultural and religious identity, the struggle for nation-
hood and the pooling of economic resources represent efforts
to develop community power; efforts that have been used
by Jewish citizens to attain their individual and collective
aspirations.

Similarly, it is increasingly urgent for Black Americans to
acquire a new sense of identity, an awareness of their own
subculture in order to really achieve a sense of community.
The Congress of Racial Equality is working for a society in
which all men are equal and respected; a goal that can only
be accomplished through the recognition of this identity and
the subsequent development of community power.

Consultative bodies between the two groups will serve a
useful end. Since the Jewish community enjoys greater status
and greater assimilation within the major society, and at the
same time has a greater depth of understanding of discrimination and oppression, it is in a unique position to work
with the Negro and the broader community for the welfare
and well-being of all Americans.

Moreover, Jews should use their influence as members of white communities to initiate and support fair housing laws and press for equal opportunity in employment and quality education for Black Americans. Too much stress is being placed on group conflicts, rather than on cooperative efforts. Such concentration can only do a disservice to both groups.

ARYEH NEIER

LARGELY BECAUSE of historical and contemporary anti-Semitism, Jews do not figure prominently in the heavy industries that are at the heart of American economic life. Excepting that small group of German Jews who acquired great wealth in investment banking, Jewish wealth in the United States has largely been acquired in soft goods manufacturing, retail merchandising and ownership of rental properties.

As a consequence, urban "have-not" Negroes have had an unusually high degree of contact with monied Jews. Negroes work for Jews as semi-skilled workers in garment factories. They purchase most of their worldly possessions from retail stores owned by Jews. They live in tenement apartments belonging to Jewish landlords who lived in the same tenements before they moved to Great Neck.

When Negro children go to school in New York City, they are more often than not taught by Jewish teachers. The chances are high that a Jewish caseworker will be assigned to a Negro family on welfare. When a Negro is ill or needs a tooth pulled, he is likely to go to a Jewish doctor or dentist. When he gets into trouble, he may need the assistance of a Jewish attorney.

Throughout an urban American Negro's life, a substantial number of the figures of authority that he meets are Jews. It would, therefore, be cause for little surprise, if the frustrations felt by Negroes at their position at the bottom of America's social heap were to produce resentment directed against those most visibly at the top, the Jews.

In fact, a recent study conducted by the Anti-Defamation League made it very clear that the preponderance of Negro sentiment was more favorable toward Jews than to whites in general. Presumably, the reason can be deduced from one of the statistics in the ADL study: 45 percent of all Negroes thought that Jews were more interested in advancing the welfare of Negroes than other whites. Only 3 percent thought that Jews were less interested in advancing Negro welfare than other whites.

It is against this background that recent reports of Negro-Jewish hostility must be viewed. There is little question but that Jews have reacted very sharply to evidence of Negro anti-Semitism. The decline and fall of the Congress of Racial Equality (CORE) as a major civil rights organization is probably more attributable to the reaction of Jewish contributors to a widely publicized anti-Semitic outburst by a CORE spokesman in Mount Vernon, New York, than even to the disaffection caused by the Black Power slogan.

As I write, New York City is in the throes of a referendum campaign on police review boards. Ordinarily, it would be hard to imagine Jews, in any sizable numbers, voting against civilian review of complaints against police. But polls conducted at early stages in the referendum campaign make it clear that Jews are less enthusiastic about civilian review than the community at large. It is difficult to interpret this phenomenon in any way other than as a symptom of an extraordinary Jewish backlash.

That Jews should react sharply to even a small amount of evidence of Negro anti-Semitism is, of course, no cause for surprise. Anti-Semitism has been too powerful and dangerous a scourge in too recent memory to permit any indications of it to be dismissed lightly. And, of course, given the prominent role that Jews have played in the advancement of the cause of Negro equality, there is a natural tendency to find the Negro anti-Semite not only dangerous but an ingrate.

But Jewish backlash against Negro anti-Semitism, however justifiable in the light of Jewish history, is hardly calculated to improve matters. Negroes, conscious of the killings, beatings, and jailings suffered by other Negroes purely for reasons of their race, must find it difficult to appreciate the sensitivity with which Jews react to an occasional anti-Semitic epithet uttered by a Negro. Given this state of affairs, it is difficult to project any rosy future for Negro-Jewish relations. Two groups in American society with long histories of persecution seem destined to grow further and further apart. While relatively little progress has been achieved, the movement for Negro equality has, for most Americans and for most Jews, lost its moral urgency. Except in the unlikely event that the Civil Rights Movement is soon again infused with the ethical spirit that was its hallmark from 1960-1965, Negro-Jewish relations seem to face a bleak future.

Would that it were possible to advocate a way out of the vicious cycle of growing anti-Negro sentiment and Negro anti-Semitism. The sentiments on both sides are simultaneously rational and irrational. They may be combatted at their rational level while no impact is made on their irrational base. Perhaps the cruelest trick of a prejudiced society is to make the victims of prejudice quarrel among themselves.

MAURICE SAMUEL

IF THE Negro freedom movement is not understood as the greatest and most fateful challenge confronting American civilization, it is not understood at all, and then no discussion of its meaning and development can yield any practical result. Without this premise an intelligible evaluation of Negro-white relations, and, more specifically, of Negro-Jewish relations, is impossible.

Accepting the premise, I would comment as follows, though not in strict order, on the questions of the symposium.

In this revolution, which has only just begun, and will cer-

tainly need not less time and labor than the revolution from
the crude capitalist state to the welfare state, there will be
many phases. In the current phase there *has* been a pronounced anti-Jewish aspect in the Negro ghetto riots, and
there *is* a Jewish backlash to Negro anti-Semitism (as well
as Jewish participation in the general backlash). Both of
these are part of the stupid inevitabilities inherent in mass
interactions when vital issues are at stake. But when something stupidly inevitable and harmful happens, we must try
to mitigate its effects, and we must begin by distinguishing
between the immediate or triggering cause and remoter, more
intractable causes.

Certainly the Jews are disproportionately represented in
the ownership of low-cost (read "slum") housing and in
retail distribution in Harlem, to begin with. But Jews are
disproportionately represented in retail distribution everywhere (I do not know whether this is true of low-cost housing everywhere). But what does "disproportionately" imply?
That we try to institute, as suggested, a "voluntary" *num-
erus clausus* on Jewish retail businesses in Negro areas? I
doubt the feasibility of the suggestion, I question its advisa-
bility on other grounds. We shall be adding to Jewish resentments by the application of a dubious principle without
bettering the Negro condition; for it is not at all evident that
the Negro buyer will be benefited by the substitution of other
white shopkeepers, or, for that matter, and as things are now,
of Negro shopkeepers. What is needed is a rapid extension of
the program, in which the American Jewish Congress is par-
ticipating, for the training and equipping of Negro retail
merchants.

The increase of anti-Semitism among Negroes has, in my
opinion, less to do with Jewish shopkeepers and slum landlords in Negro areas than with wider, deeper and more general factors. The parallel between the Negro and the Jewish
condition in the past used to express itself in songs like "Let
My People Go." The contrast between the Negro and the
Jewish condition in present-day America expresses itself in
the transference of the word "ghetto" from the Jew to the
Negro. Always and everywhere Jewish success and affluence
provoke envy, suspicion and hostility; in the context of our

problem Negro frustrations are bound to seek this outlet, and with added vehemence (I ignore the endemic anti-Semitism of Christendom). The injustice and futility of it must not, in turn, affect our affirmative attitude toward Negro emancipation.

There is something revoltingly coarse in the snarl one sometimes hears from Jews: "Look, we came here poor and despised. We won through by our own efforts. Let the Negroes do the same." I need not enter into the total falseness of the analogy. I will only remark that nowhere does success justify an offensive and taunting attitude of moral superiority.

In any case the backlash among Jews as among non-Jews is an ugly dishonesty. Every excuse that can be found for the repudiation of the irksome duty—and the rectification of the Negro wrong means nothing more than that to many people— will be eagerly seized upon and inflated into a huge issue. No sooner had the slogan "Black Power" been coined than the alarm was sounded. Before it was ascertained what the slogan might actually mean, before any investigation was made as to the proportion of Negroes who read into it an extremist, racist interpretation, the worst was assumed. I suggest that the quite senseless notions attached by extremist Negro leaders to the slogan no more represent the Negro liberation movement as a whole than the Sternists did the Zionist movement. This is not to say that such extremism may be ignored, any more than the Sternists could be ignored; but to bring it up as a pretext for diminished support of the Negro emancipation calls to mind certain Jews—and non-Jews—who used to say regarding the Sternists: "If that is what Zionism leads to, we wash our hands of it" (actually there was nothing to wash). Every year such people withdrew from us the support they had not given us the year before. An urgent freedom movement without violent extremists in it has never existed; and if murder goes unpunished why should only Negroes be expected not to kill? The record shows that white violence against Negroes far outweighs Negro violence against whites—proof that herein the Negro is in advance of the white in fitness for citizenship. Not that Negro violence can be condoned; it must be fought, repressed, discouraged; but the movement must not suffer for it.

As to whether Jews owe a special ethical debt to the Negro

liberation movement, I would say that I recognize no grada-
tions of obligation. Actually Jews *are* more sensitive to the
issue; on the other hand they are terribly and understandably
sensitive to manifestations of anti-Semitism. No one can say
whether Jews or Negroes have suffered more at the hands of
white Christian civilization (against the pogroms and the
death-ovens set the stinking slaveships on which hundreds of
thousands of Negroes died like vermin—and there are other
parallels), but Jews should make a desperate effort to keep
the historic perspective before their eyes. They are the natural allies of the Negroes; they must look on Negro anti-Semitism as part of the Negro tragedy; they must not let themselves
be deflected by it, however much it stings, from the pursuit of
a common aim, which is the leveling of differences in the
rights and privileges of groups.

Whether the Rabbinate and the Jewish lay organizations
have contributed their "proper" share to the Negro liberation
movement is again a question that has no answer. There is no
"proper" share, for the support of the movement is among
those *mitzvot* which are classified as *ein lahem shiyur*, there is
no limit to their claim on us. My impression is that the Rabbinate and the lay organizations have done proportionately at
least as much as the non-Jewish clergy and laity.

It is also my impression that the Negro leaders have *not*
done their full duty or anything like it in counteracting anti-
Semitism among Negroes. I am not aware that they have
explained to their constituency, with clarity and insistence,
that anti-Semitism is the enemy of the Negro as well as of the
Jew; that it not only degrades the Negro liberation movement
morally, but is a windfall for white extreme rightists, which
they use to play Jew and Negro off against each other to the
injury of both; that it is the classical trap set by reactionaries
for oppressed masses in revolt; that, specifically, it poisons the
springs of the religious element which has been so prominent
and ennobling a feature of the liberation movement.

I do not think it would be helpful to establish Negro-Jewish
consultative bodies to examine misunderstandings, etc. Individual Jews may and should talk with individual Negroes on
this and other problems. Jewish organizations may and should
have a special program of participation in the Negro liberation

movement, and to that extent there will be useful contacts, and a certain clarification will follow. But special consultative Negro-Jewish bodies on Negro anti-Semitism would create the impression of Jews bargaining with Negroes, whereas our support should be unconditional. Consultative bodies should be created, and they should consist of Negroes, white non-Jews and Jews. They should be concerned with anti-Semitism *not* as a Jewish but as an American and generally human problem.

The historic perspective which Jewish and Negro leadership should keep before their eyes in the liberation movement brings out a tragic and instructive parallel. Around the turn of the century the perilous situation of the Jews of Eastern Europe was sharply aggravated by events in Rumania and Russia, and the cry went up from Zionists: "We want a Jewish homeland *now*." We wanted it and needed it because we felt greater disasters approaching. The slogan took on flesh in the great Uganda error (one thinks with something like horror of the possibility that there might, today, have been a Jewish state imbedded in Central Africa) to which Herzl and many of his followers succumbed in a moment of despair. We wanted and needed a Jewish homeland then, but it was unobtainable. Against the anguished but futile cry, which took on added shrillness after the Kishinev and other pogroms, Weizmann and his followers offered the bitter and realistic advice: "We shall not get a Jewish homeland anywhere without great preparation from within."

A generation later the need was infinitely more desperate. We would not have saved all the six million even if by then the Jewish State had been a reality; but there would have been an enormous difference. We had to stand by and watch the calamity almost helplessly because we were not sufficiently prepared, and however we might scream: "Jewish homeland *now!*" the realities could not be changed. It was only after the great calamity that the patient work of the preceding generation bore fruit.

The ultimate triumph of the Negro liberation movement will be the result of cumulative interaction between rising Negro education and increasing white concessions. I use "education" in the widest sense, to include the schools of America and the schooling of Negroes in political and social action.

No one will hand them freedom on a silver platter, as no one handed a homeland to the Jews, *and that is the relevance of the "Black Power" slogan.* Like the Zionist movement of yesterday, the Negroes are caught in a vicious circle. The Jews could not get a homeland till they had proved they could build one, and that they could not prove because they were not given the chance. Negroes justly demand that opportunity should be available to them on equal terms with whites; but their demand will only be met as they acquire the education which is denied them.

In life, vicious circles which cannot be broken can often be corroded, and this is what is happening, or beginning to happen (but with what miserable slowness!) in Negro education. The inertia of indifference and the brake of hostility slow up the process, and of the two the first is perhaps the more disheartening, for it represents a large mass, and it is so easily stirred to hostility. If we ignore the serious aspect of school "bussing" (whether it serves a good purpose to bring Negro children artificially into a white neighborhood and its school), what a pitiable row was raised by white parents about the "inconvenience" of the proposal, as though thousands of white children did not use busses regularly to go to private schools. "We are absolutely in favor of helping the Negro toward equality, but please, don't become a nuisance about it."

I return to the parallel with the bloodless social revolution from primitive capitalism to the welfare state. Less than fifty years ago, here in America, the social assumptions (still far from perfect) now prevailing would have seemed not merely Utopian to the large majority of well-to-do Americans, but immoral, subversive of initiative, destructive of the sterling qualities which built up our country. Today the welfare state is self-understood as the proper, the becoming, the inevitable thing for a great, affluent country—self-understood, of course, except for the still unreconstructed troglodytes who hanker for the evil old times. Less than fifty years hence, I believe, equality of place for the Negro in our society will, for the great majority, be a tacitly accepted reality—though then also the warped hungerers for domination will be lamenting the disappearance of the "heroic past." But again, how much labor and persistence is going to be needed for this transformation, and what a change of outlook in the millions who look upon the Negro liberation movement as just "one of those political things."

STEVEN S. SCHWARZSCHILD

THE PROBLEMS of Negro-Jewish relations must be put in their proper frame of reference before they can be analyzed usefully for Jewish purposes. That frame of reference is, perforce, a religio-theological and an ethical one. Sociological, historical and political considerations must find their subordinate place within such a scheme.

The religiously Jewish values that are substantially relevant to such an analysis may be held, briefly, to be the following: 1) Judaism is committed with its full weight to striving for the good society—"to repair the world by means of the Kingdom of Heaven"; 2) this striving in Judaism for the good society is not only a social or even a philosophical but a divine imperative and must, therefore, be enacted in a radical fashion—i.e., it demands attitudes and actions in accord with the revolutionary aim of establishing the Kingdom of God on earth and in accord with the revolutionary methods toward that aim indicated in Jewish law and ethics; 3) considerations of race in the determination of social values and policies not only run counter to such aspirations, but also violate the most fundamental principles and sensibilities of the Jewish ethos; 4) in the Jewish scheme of redemption, Negroes and Jews obviously play different roles in the economy of the coming of the Kingdom: Negroes are simply part of the human race as a whole, and no special responsibilities devolve upon them anymore than upon any other group of people—other than Israel, who are chosen as the specific instrument through which the Kingdom is to be brought about and who, therefore,

labor under responsibilities not imposed on others—"Therefore did the Holy One, blessed be He, multiply teaching and
commandments for Israel."

From these premises a number of conclusions which have a
direct, practical bearing on Negro-Jewish relations in America
today immediately follow.

For one thing, Negroes—and others—are entirely right
when they expect immensely higher standards of behavior from
Jews than from anyone else: "You only have I chosen from all
the families of the earth; therefore will I requite from you all
your sins." The Jew, when he acts only in conformity with
human conventions, falls short of divine law and betrays the
interests of the Messianic Kingdom. Therefore, when Jewish
landlords and storekeepers in Harlem and Watts, for example,
suffer more painfully in riots than their non-Jewish neighbors,
this is not only a consequence of quite obvious socio-histori-
cal causes but also and primarily the punishing and challenging "rod of God's anger," which the entire Jewish community
should heed.

In the second place, the widespread Jewish reaction to
Negro anti-Semitism can be seen, on our premises, to be
entirely mistaken, even religiously suicidal. To draw any
analogies between Negro and Jewish fate, Negro and Jewish
suffering, is to disregard the fundamental difference that Israel
always undergoes its experiences "for the sake of Heaven,"
i.e., with meaning and purpose, however incomprehensible and
infinitely catastrophic these may be. The suffering which
Negroes undergo on the other hand is due to entirely trivial
and accidental causes of pigment and economics, and is therefore intolerable. To suffer and to be disadvantaged for the
sake of God is one thing—to be forced to suffer and be disadvantaged absurdly is in one sense, a much more unbearable
and obnoxious condition.

To conclude from some manifestations of Negro anti-
Semitism that Jews are justified in "taking their marbles and
going home" from the civil rights struggle is thus merely
another symptom of such a false analogy. Israel is not in this
game on a "tit-for-tat" basis. Were this the case, we would
have had to abandon the striving for mankind's good life a
long time ago. We must continue to enact an attitude of com-

plete color-blindness and a dedication to the total abolition of social injustices, regardless of the cost to us.

The general impression is that Jews have been identified in history with "the oppressed." This is theologically correct, but historically the opposite has always been a temptation and often a reality. In medieval Europe, for example, Jews sought and frequently found protection from emperors and kings and were then identified with them when peasants, guilds, and urban commercial interests rebelled against them in the pursuit of broader social vistas. Similar conditions prevailed where European colonialists, in North Africa, for instance, used Jews —and Jews let themselves be used—as buffers between themselves and the indigenous population. The tool, willing or unwilling, that is used in and benefits from oppression cannot complain when it is attacked together with the oppression. Two lessons must be learned by Jews from this consideration: in the first place, there is no use protesting that we were in Lithuania when slavery was practiced in this country—we did not reject the advantages of being "white" in a white country during the last century. More broadly, we should always weigh the immediate benefits that various "establishments" offer us against our long-range moral commitments, even if the latter may meanwhile be detrimental to us.

Now the question is where do we go from here. Symposia, "goodwill" organizations, declarations of friendship and support are nearly useless. Jewish history has proved their vanity. Also the Negro community has had a superfluity of them; it demands proof in action. Above all, the God of Israel is not on record as a God of resolutions, or a God of goodwill dinners, but as the God "who upholds the falling, heals the sick, and liberates the imprisoned." The Civil Rights Movement and messianic Judaism are at one, in that their aim is not delayed and partial, but complete and immediate: we are committed, body and soul, to the good society, all of it, now, here and everywhere. Action, both individual and collective, is imperative—total, revolutionary action. The Jewish program must, therefore, be in effect messianic, with all that this implies. Such a stand would speak incomparably more eloquently to the Negro community than well-intentioned conferences. It will be more radical and more Jewish than anything that even

the most militant sectors of the Negro community have as yet
conceived—and we would no longer be open to the accusation
that we are trying to ingratiate ourselves. Negroes are learning
the same lesson that surely the Holocaust has taught Jewry:
Christian, white, Western culture has no room for the ethics
that issue forth from where Africa and Asia conjoin. For Jews
and Negroes common action is, therefore, not only a policy of
good tactics in this hour of world history but, above all, the
call of their ethos and cultures.

BEN B. SELIGMAN

BEFORE TRYING to respond to the questions the editors
have posed it would appear useful to assess the relative positions of Jews and Negroes in America today. Some members
of our affluent society, especially those who might have experienced rough times in their youth, are apt to be bemused
by the concern in recent years over such issues as poverty, the
Negro ghetto, hard-core unemployment and the like. No one,
they say, legislated a war on poverty or the defense of civil
rights for Irish, Italian and Jewish immigrants at the turn of
the century. Faced by a hostile environment that was nevertheless filled with opportunity, these ethnic groups overcame
their bewilderment, seized the main chance, and climbed the
ladder of success, The Irish gained political pre-eminence in
Massachusetts, the Italians were able to fuse their home country heritage with new American values, the Jews achieved
economic heights that almost matched those of the white
Anglo-Saxon Protestant. If there are poor people around us
today—and so many of them are Negroes—then it must be
due to defects of character, lack of will, or unwillingness to
undertake risk.

What is not acknowledged, however, is that poverty and
urban degradation today have a new shape, a physiognomy

that is substantially different from what existed fifty or sixty years ago. The older poverty through which immigrant Irish and destitute Jews passed was an accompaniment to the unfolding of industrial expansion. Not much more pleasant to be sure than today's poverty, it was at least surrounded by a layer of hope. Not only were there burgeoning industries to absorb the newcomer—steel, railroads, textiles, clothing—but the economy's need for sheer muscle power obviated any prospective demand for great skill or education. Not only were job opportunities plentiful, but even more important, there was a kind of internal ladder of opportunity that allowed a young man to climb, for example, all the way from floorsweeper to skilled machinist in not too many years. There were enough such instances to lend a measure of reality to the American promise.

What of the Negro? The elimination of slavery had done little to improve his lot. While he no longer was subjected to what had been undoubtedly the worst form of slavery the world had ever seen, he was soon shackled by rigid Jim Crow laws that defined his status for years to come in terms of a caste system which revealed economic, social and even sexual overtones. To escape Southern oppression, akin to a gigantic concentration camp, the Negro moved northward, a migration that reached flood proportions after World War II. Yet even in the North, he was confined to certain neighborhoods that quickly acquired the seventeenth century name of "ghetto." These ghettos had no walls but their inhabitants were compressed by social and economic barriers that served as well as brick and mortar.

Here were people without power, and white society—of which the Jew is part—saw to it that they remained without power. The consequence was a condition of pathologic isolation, creating a poverty subculture that threatened to dehumanize the Negro. Given the worst housing, suffering the same discrimination to which he had been subjected in the South, offered only unskilled work, it was not surprising that the Negro's reaction should be aggressive, rebellious and self-destructive. What indeed can white society expect when thousands of persons are cramped into houses built almost a hundred years ago and are then required to pay rentals often providing a 100 percent annual return on the landlord's investment? What indeed can white society expect when shoddy goods are sold on the installment plan to ghetto families at interest rates far exceeding legal limits? What indeed can white society expect when Negro craftsmen are not permitted to pursue their trades? What indeed can we expect when the Negro is denied access to decent education, denied the same wages as whites, compressed into tighter and tighter quarters by "urban renewal," made to suffer a higher death rate?

The resentment of the Negro against the manner in which white America had forced him into an economic and social vise was bound to explode into violence. The riots we have witnessed across the nation really constitute a change in the attitudes of Negroes. These riots are not local phenomena by any means, but rather an expression of deep-seated social impatience that extends three thousand miles from Watts to Harlem. They are a form of bargaining with white society, a form that stems from the desperation engendered by discrimination, poverty and hopelessness. In many instances, the major thrust of the violence has been toward the police and the local merchant, one a symbol of political oppression, the other a symbol of economic oppression. And in the latter the Jew represents in the Negro's mind an important component.

To assert that the Jewish merchant accounts for a "minute share of Negro economic misery," may perhaps be correct, but it is beside the point. For the Jewish merchant and landlord is the *visible* symbol of the Negro's agony, and that is what the Negro seeks to destroy. By expunging merchant and landlord from his existence, the Negro expunges the white man. To be sure, the Negro community feuds with other white groups as well: in Chicago, Negroes quarrel with the dominant Irish and Polish groups over the school system and in Boston a similar issue smolders when an open segregationist is elected to the School Committee. But who owned most of the stores on 125th St. in Harlem? Or who was it that rented to him run-down shacks at exorbitant rates in New Orleans and Norfolk? I fear that the identification of the Jew by the Negro as landlord-merchant is one of long duration.

The disparity between Jew and Negro in America is great, perhaps so great as to cast into doubt any reconciliation of the two groups that have suffered most at the hands of others. Jews, like most immigrants to America prior to World War II, have done well; the Negro, an internal immigrant, is still at the bottom of the economic ladder. A study of Jewish economic characteristics I made a number of years ago (as part of a broader study of Jewish demography) showed that perhaps a third of Jewish heads of households were self-employed, that from a third to a half were in the wholesale-retail trades, and that the proportion of proprietors and managers among Jews far exceed the ratio to be found in the total white population. The data also suggested that most Jewish retailers were to be found in groceries, apparel, shoes, furniture, and hardware— precisely those lines most common in what are now the Negro ghettos. This is not to say that Jews specifically selected such neighborhoods for their ventures; with the shift in population, with the flight of whites to suburbia, the Jewish businessman simply found that he had new customers. And the latter were totally unaccustomed to the ways of petty business to be found in local neighborhoods.

Why do we delude ourselves? To a businessman—any white businessman—the Negro's money, when he has it, is "second class" money. It never buys the same services as the white customer with the same amount to spend. Moreover, the Negro who came recently to the big city ghettos from the South, can recall that the businessman with whom he had dealt in New Orleans, Norfolk, or Atlanta, was apt to be a Jew. It is little wonder that he quickly identified much of his economic suffering with those Jewish merchants and landlords he met in the North. What will it mean to the Negro to be told that discrimination and unwillingness to offer employment stem mainly from the large corporations? If the latter are far removed from immediacy for the general run of common folk, how abstract are they for residents of the ghetto? No, I fear no amount of statistics about retail ownership, installment selling or real estate will prevent the Negro from equating Whitey with Goldberg. The misery he suffers is Goldberg's.

The point is not for Jews to avoid Harlem, but rather to be concerned with such neighborhoods as communities. Unappetizing retraining programs with vague promises of employment attached to them are hardly adequate. Where transportation is essential—as in Watts—the Jewish organizations might try to lend their community expertise in this unfamiliar area of need, for without public transportation in and out of Watts, jobs are difficult to find and hold. Or Negroes might be encouraged to set up retail businesses. Of course, there would be competition from established firms; but more seriously, it is doubtful that Negroes can secure the necessary capital. While the element of risk ought to be weighed alike for black and white, most banks consider a Negro businessman to be marginal. As in many another walk of life business success is an important symbol of achievement, but the Negro is usually denied the chance to pursue that goal. The real prospect for a Negro business is a tiny retail store with inadequate resources for building inventory or improving marketing techniques and wholly dependent on family labor. White society says the Negro is a poor businessman and then proves its case by preventing him from demonstrating otherwise.

If Jews, who have a long history of community organization, want to foster improved relationships with Negroes, they might fruitfully pursue the channels of development suggested above. That should do more to cement good relationships than the insensate urgings of "war on poverty" workers to strive and to adopt willy-nilly middle-class values. Obviously, Negroes wouldn't reject such values if the middle-class economy and middle-class opportunities were open to them. Social stability and social advancement in this context means a genuinely open society: in the absence of the latter only continued turmoil can result. And Jews do not prosper in turmoil.

WILLIAM STRINGFELLOW

PERHAPS THE most poignant dimension of the American racial crisis, especially in the Northern cities, is the surfacing of anti-Semitism among some Negro citizens.

Negro anti-Semitism is not of recent origin. It is not a new or sudden phenomenon. It has been latent in the urban black ghettos for a very long time, but only lately has become conspicuous.

Pickets have denounced Jewish investment in slum tenements. There have been boycotts of some Jewish merchants and many stores owned by Jews in the ghettos have suffered looting during the race riots. At least one—though not all—of the black nationalist sects openly preaches anti-Semitism, and it is frequently rumored that it receives financial support from other anti-Semites, like the American Nazi Party. In one community, a furor was caused by an anti-Semitic remark of a prominent Negro in a public meeting—though the press generally overlooked the fact that the speaker was provoked by an anti-Negro slur uttered by a Jew. Anti-Semitic epithets can be found splashed across signs and fences and the sides of buildings in the black slums. Certain celebrity Negroes are ridiculed openly by their own people as "black Jews" or "bought Negroes"—Sammy Davis Jr., for example, as one Negro said to me not long ago, "may be the most popular Negro among the Jews but he is the most unpopular Jew among the Negroes."

There is a terrible irony in Negro anti-Semitism, since both the Jews and the American Negroes have inheritances of rejection and exile. Both have long endured, and still do, both vicious and vulgar discrimination and subtle, de facto separation in many sectors of American life. The irony is compounded, too, by the truth that American Jews have been more generous in their concern for and support of civil rights than any other single group, religious or ethnic, within the white community in America. Moreover, unlike so many whites, the Jews exercised a social witness on behalf of American Negroes decades before the Negro revolution gained organic significance and its present prominence.

If many American Jews are astonished and hurt because Negro anti-Semites are not duly appreciative of the pioneering role of Jews in civil rights for Negroes and for all citizens, there is perhaps a partial explanation in the peril of whites acting paternalistically while advocating equality for Negroes.

Moreover, there are some facts which help explain, if not condone, Negro anti-Semitism. In New York City, for example, where there are about two and a half million Jews and approximately a million Negroes, the Jews were long retarded in their political emergence because of the hostility of other white immigrants and natives. But now that they have received some political recognition and achieved some significant political power, Negro New Yorkers have begun to stir and organize and assert their own claim to political attention and tribute. Thus Jews and Negroes become direct competitors in city politics, a circumstance unlikely to endear one to the other.

Another facet to the issue is the legacy of discrimination against Jews in the business and investment communities which restricted the areas in which they could purchase property or the enterprises which they could undertake. Hence there are numerous stores and many slum tenements in the black ghettos owned and controlled by Jews, though let it be emphasized that there is plenty of slum real estate owned by other white people and by banks, insurance companies, universities, unions, churches and other institutional powers.

White Protestants and white Catholics may find it easy to behold the outbreak of Negro anti-Semitism as a matter of concern only to Negroes and Jews, as something which, if it is to be absolved, is the exclusive responsibility of Negroes and Jews.

If white Christians embrace that escape, they will be both dishonest and stupid. Dishonest because it has been white Christians, historically, in America as in some other countries, who have made anti-Semitism a badge of the establishment in society, a status mark distinguishing the "ins" from the "outs" in politics, business, in many of the arts, in much of private education, in social rank, in housing and residency. It should not be surprising that some Negroes, aspiring to acceptance in contemporary society, emulate the anti-Semitism of white Christians. Stupid because the hostility evident in Negro anti-Semitism can only have its fruition in the enmity of black citizens for all white men, not alone the Jews.

Negro anti-Semitism puts Jews and Negroes into conflict, but it places white Christians in an even more excruciating position because it exposes so plainly and so woefully their guilt and their apostasy: their gruesome blame for the turmoil which engulfs this nation.

MARIE SYRKIN

ANY DISCUSSION of Negro-Jewish relations assumes that there is a relationship to be explored. Though no ethnic, religious or cultural bonds exist between Jews and Negroes, the frequent, sometimes nervous, juxtaposition of these two groups suggests a kinship, perhaps in fate if not in history. Under discussion in this symposium is not the obligation which Jews share with all Americans to participate to their utmost in the Negro liberation movement—an obligation which no liberal would dispute. (I use the term "liberal" advisedly, since despite the derision the term has lately enjoyed no adequate substitute for the ideological stance it represents is available.) Implicit is the suggestion that Jews have a particular responsibility as Jews. For this reason I shall begin with Question 7—"Do Jews because of the ethics of their religion and because of their historical experience as a persecuted group owe a special debt of greater participation in the Negro liberation movement than their Christian neighbors?" —as its formulation provides a rationale for the subject posed.

I am not prepared to measure the degree to which Jewish ethics imposes greater moral obligations than Christian ethics. Both religions abound in pronouncements on the brotherhood of man and challenging ethical precepts. If in practice a strikingly high percentage of Jews commit themselves to causes advocating social justice, their ledger should show credit rather than debt. The Jewish embrace of the visions of Isaiah, Marx, or Moses Hess may be the natural characteristic of an oppressed, spiritually ardent people, as is Jewish readiness for involvement and for mounting the barri-

cades. In 1966 I wryly salute the Jew in his classic role of
heir of the prophets, but while I commend him I reject the
notion that his is a command performance; the part should
be played at will and with some regard for audience response.

There then remains the second half of the question: Do
Jews have a special obligation because of their experience as
a persecuted minority? Since the common element between
Negro and Jew is membership in a disadvantaged minority, it is
not irrelevant to point out that every form of discrimination,
segregation and physical violence to which Negroes have been
subjected has been endured in more terrible and overwhelm-
ing measure by Jews in our time. Some Negroes, suspecting
odious comparisons, resent such reminders; however, to rede-
fine the area of common ground is no impertinence. The meta-
phors of the Negro revolution recognize the parallels, whether
in spirituals, "Let My People Go," or in the adoption of a vo-
cabulary ("ghetto") from specific Jewish experience, medieval
and modern.

Now to the question: Does Jewish experience, past and current, constitute a "debt"? Does a burden, doffed in the United
States and, lately, in some parts of Europe, require the assumption of additional burdens on the theory that the heavy-laden
have stronger and more willing backs than their luckier fellows?

A rhetorical question provides its answer. At the same time,
while I do not believe that Jews have a special *duty* rising
out of their history, I accept the idea that their special *experience* has given Jews a unique understanding of the role of
a minority in a given society, and that this understanding enables them to differentiate with some authority between the possible and impossible, legitimate and illegitimate, goals that a
minority may set itself. Of course, Jews have no business to
offer unwanted counsel, but insofar as they espouse the Negro
struggle they should determine on the basis of their expert
knowledge which of its aspects invites their support. Precisely
because they are so thoroughly acquainted with the whole
spectrum of prejudice they can permit themselves a critical
evaluation rather than a blanket endorsement, and they can
do so without fearing that they fail in sympathy or com-
prehension.

A minority seeking to preserve its cultural and religious identity, while sharing in the political, economic and intellectual life of a society on equal terms with other citizens, must maintain a delicate balance between feasible and unfeasible demands. Jews have consistently interpreted emancipation as meaning equal civil rights and free access to the opportunities offered by a given society, to be enjoyed in accordance with their abilities. If in the exercise of these rights and opportunities they noted that most of their associates in schools and neighborhoods were Jews, none except assimilationists viewed such fellowship as a diminution of privilege or dignity. Progress was measured by the possibilities for education and the quality of the home life, neither of which depended on the creed or complexion of those who shared the classroom or street. Social and economic advance followed rapidly upon the fall of legal barriers. Once the quota system was formally disavowed, the immigrant neighborhood school became the portal for universities, from City College to Harvard. While indifferent to the ethnic homogeneity of their surroundings, Jews unremittingly fought any attempt at legal discrimination and they certainly would not have accepted any which enforced residence in a "pale" or which set up special "Jewish" regulations for school admission. The same pattern obtains more or less for the other minorities in the United States. They develop within the framework of basic assumptions of American democracy; hence the assertion and preservation of these assumptions becomes for them both a matter of principle and of self-interest. There is no realistic indication that the Negro minority will be able to progress outside of this pattern.

Negro leaders cite the reluctance of "white liberals," Jews among them, to support some of their demands and tactics in the North, as evidence of unreliability when the chips are down: it is easier to applaud from afar than to accept the consequences of the Negro revolution nearer home. This interpretation is too easy. Much of the murk which now clouds relations between white and Negro civil rights advocates rises from the transformation of simplistic slogans into alarmingly confused goals. The most dangerous of these is the apparent readiness of militant Negro groups, indignant at de facto segregation, to seek the institution of a willed segregation on the grounds that the difference between de facto and legal segregation is merely semantic. This equation is superficial and misleading. Those who uncritically preach its truth, not only imperil present gains but reverse the course of Negro emancipation.

The Negro mobile "ghetto" is not the walled-in enclosure the word denotes. Anyone familiar with residential patterns in New York City, for instance, knows that during the last twenty years highly desirable sections of the city have changed from middle-class Irish or Jewish to Negro and Puerto Rican. The departure, however reprehensible, of the original house-owners or tenants does not alter the crucial fact of mobility. The same process has taken place in other urban centers in the North, and the local school inevitably reflects the changed composition of the neighborhood.

Obviously, communities harmoniously mixed in carefully balanced proportions might be preferable, but New York, outside of the redoubt of Harlem, already bears witness that even de facto segregation is increasingly fluid. The middle-class, integrated apartment house in which I live on Manhattan's West Side is flanked by Negro and white streets in no predictable pattern. Under these circimstances to protest the mobile, open "ghetto" is meaningless. The energy were better expended on preventing the deterioration of the new localities by raising the economic and social level of the community. Withdrawal into the mythical domain of Black Power will not provide employment or greater educational opportunities.

The same holds good in the matter of schools, now perhaps the most explosive issue in the North. The parent who is sickened by the spectacle of white thugs attacking Negro children going to school in Grenada is not guilty of hypocrisy if he objects to the forcible bussing of his child out of the neighborhood in which he lives. In Manhattan, for example, where the majority of the school population is Negro and Puerto Rican, no mathematical sleight-of-hand can prevent de facto segregation unless white children are imported from other boroughs. In a democratic society all that a member of an ethnic minority may sensibly demand is the non-discriminatory application of the rules according to which its institutions operate. He is justified in demanding the best possible education the school can offer but he can no more require the presence of white pupils than a white parent can demand the exclusion of Negro pupils in some other neighborhood. The right is to the school, not the pupils; to the neighborhood, not the neighbors.

To the extent that Jews are affected by the "white backlash," they are engaged in re-evaluating the new direction of the Civil Rights Movement and deciding how far they are prepared to follow. Till the emergence of the Black Power extremists, the goals and means of the Negro movement were those traditionally acceptable to white liberals. The right to vote, the right to the undiscriminatory use of every public facility from schools to parks to subways, the right to jobs and decent housing, required no exposition for their espousal. Disenchantment, for whites as well as Negroes, came when the Negro movement began to change not only the means but the basic assumptions as to the goals to be sought. The controversy (with distinct anti-Semitic overtones) around Intermediate School 201 in Harlem is a concrete illustration of a trend in the wrong direction.

The new school is superbly equipped and has a first-rate teaching staff, including some thirty Negro teachers. Provision has been made for small classes and individual teaching—in other words, P.S. 201 is a showcase school both in its physical plant and its educational planning. However, instead of being hailed, the school has been vociferously picketed because of de facto segregation: white parents predictably refused to have their children bussed to Harlem. A Harlem committee has demanded the dismissal of the white principal, a Jew. This last bit of information is not irrelevant since one of the picketers shouted, "We got too many teachers and principals named Ginzberg and Rosenberg in Harlem." (*The New York Times*, Sept. 13, 1966.) The indignation of the faculty at this demand, caused the principal to rescind his offer to resign. The hubbub continues, with Negro leaders insisting on varying degrees of community control over the curriculum and selection of faculty, including a Negro principal.

This episode provides a clear example of the overturning of basic assumptions, an overturning whose consequences must be cautiously examined by those most concerned: namely, all vulnerable minorities. The scrapping of the merit system according to which teachers are appointed without regard to race or creed will inevitably subject the public school system to the pressures of local groups. No overactive imagination is needed to visualize what may happen if the Board of Education yields on this issue. White bigots are no less zealous than Negro extremists, and once the principle for an independent school system is abandoned in Harlem, the precedent will be set. Every ethnic and religious group will begin clamoring for the right to hire and fire teachers, and to shape the curriculum in accordance with its notions and prejudices. Despite its notable record in supporting integration, the United Teachers Federation opposes granting supervisory powers to community groups, though teachers welcome the legitimate, active involvement of the community in a consultative capacity. But the demands of the Harlem committee strike at the heart of the present egalitarian civil service system with its built-in protections against capricious and discriminatory decisions. Minorities whose chief opportunity resides in the impartial functioning of an independent public school system would be both foolhardy and unprincipled if they countenanced the weakening of traditional democratic bulwarks.

Admittedly, parochial schools, Hebrew schools, and all kinds of private schools are geared to special group interests. But these schools are not part of the public school system nor are they maintained by the state. The groups concerned, frequently at considerable financial sacrifice and effort, support their institutions. The Harlem committee, by demanding both group authority and public financing, puts forward a program injurious in the long run to every minority. Even if members of the Harlem committee were considerably more judicious and competent to deal with educational problems than they appear to be judging from their manifestoes, and even if they succeeded in enlisting the guidance of acknowledged educators, the authority over a public school should remain within the public school system.

The question of Negro anti-Semitism may be noted in this context. The usual explanation for its existence—the presence of the Jewish slumlord or exploiting merchant, "Mr. Goldberg"

—is shaken by the emergence of "Mr. Ginzberg," the Jewish principal or teacher, repudiated by the Harlem demonstrator I quoted. Whatever the sins of "Mr. Goldberg," no charge of exploitation or self-interest can be made against "Mr. Ginzberg." On the contrary, assignments to what are euphemistically described as "underprivileged areas" are generally dreaded and, if possible, shunned; only idealistic teachers seek to cope with the enormous disciplinary and educational problems presented, and they get neither additional pay nor advancement for a heavily taxing assignment. Yet "Mr. Ginzberg" gets no plaudits; he is classed with "Mr. Goldberg."

Insofar as "Mr. Goldberg" is a reality he should get out of Watts and Harlem. Jewish exploiters may be no worse than other white exponents of the business ethic, but they provide too convenient a scapegoat. "Mr. Ginzberg," on the other hand, whether in the schools or in the Civil Rights Movement, will presumably continue to act according to his lights. His presence in many guises—be it as civil rights martyr, teacher, philanthropist, or merely as a friendly Harlem druggist—will not keep some strident Negro spokesmen from adopting vulgar anti-Semitic stereotypes. Anti-Semitism, Negro and white, feeds on its own hates; its inner dynamic will not be checked by objective demonstrations no matter how irrefutably the data be marshalled. This is an old story. Nevertheless, full Negro emancipation is an American problem, and as such is Mr. Ginzberg's concern. But while he participates in its solution in whatever measure he sees fit, Ginzberg should not yield to the temptation of mouthing slogans his intelligence rejects and espousing objectives his experience recognizes as a threat to all.

GUS TYLER

NEGRO-JEWISH relationships elude an easy answer for the simple reason that neither community is monolithic. There are many Jewish communities and even more Jews. The same is true

of the Negro. Hence, there are many different kinds of relationships—some amicable, some hostile, and some indifferent.

In the realm of social action, the traditional relationship
has been a close alliance between liberal Jewry and Negro
strivings. Jews have been activists—founders, contributors and
frontline fighters—in the Civil Rights or Negro self-improve-
ment movements, whether it be the NAACP, the Urban League,
CORE, SNCC, or the Negro College Fund. The alliance was
natural between two minority groups, risen out of slavery, seeking security and opportunity in a society of tolerance and
democracy.

This traditional alliance is presently in jeopardy. Tensions
have been rising between sectors of the Negro and Jewish
communities. Although this creeping hostility has hardly grown
to such proportions as to dominate the relations between the
two groups, it is of sufficient significance to demand early analysis and action.

Present friction between sectors of the Negro and Jewish
communities arises from a dual source: first, tensions between
the Negro and the white world around him; second, tensions
within the "Negro revolution."

The reasons why Negroes are hostile to the white world
have been recorded a million times. To many Negroes of limited
experience, however, the Jew, although a tiny part of America's population, *is* the white man. "Goldberg" is "whitey" to
some Negroes, mainly to the group that has constant contact
with Jews as employers, as retailers, as mistresses of the household. Hence, Negro anger with the "white" is turned against
the "Jew," in exactly the same way that medieval discontent
with the ruling aristocracy expressed itself in pogroms against
Jews who were occasional underlings in the feudal power
structure.

Secondly, it is almost axiomatic that any group fighting its
way out of the lower depths will first of all strike out at the
ethnic (or economic) group just one head above it. Hitting the
top of the power structure is difficult since the real rulers
are too distant, too impersonal, too untouchable. It's easier to
hit the people who only until a few years ago inhabited the
neighborhood. The early gang wars of New York were led by
Irish Catholics battling their poor Protestant neighbors. The

early Jewish gangs of the East Side and East New York aimed their brass knuckles and lead bullets at the Irish. The Italian gangs drove both Irish and Jews from the streets. In this warfare, there were "riots" of massive proportions, resulting in torture, murder, pitched gun battles, and the burning down of city blocks.

Rioting that flares in the Negro ghettos today shoots its flames at all neighbors: Poles in Chicago, Italians in Cleveland, Puerto Ricans in East New York, and Jews whenever they are the nearest at hand. Unresolved anger—when expressed in terms of black versus white—is not selective: it lashes out at all whose skins are white and whose bodies are close.

In the specific cases where the Jew is the ready target, there are other factors that heighten the conflict. These factors arise from the internal struggle within the Negro "revolution."

Revolutions, no matter how heroic, are not manned by heroes only. Social upheavals attract a motley crew: theorists and terrorists, martyrs and murderers, saints and self-seekers, demi-gods and demagogues. In the heat of conflict, they appear outwardly fused by a common hatred. Yet within the maelstrom, factions are engaged in a struggle for the soul or the muscle of the movement—as in the French Revolution of 1789 (Mountain versus Jacobin), the Russian Revolution of 1917 (Bolshevik versus Menshevik) or the Spanish Civil War of 1936 (Stalinists versus Socialists). What holds for all these conflicts also holds for the Negro Revolution of the 1960's —extremists versus moderates.

To a few of the extremist elements, the attack on the Jew is a handy device. Ironically, this is so precisely because liberal Jewry has for many years been in such close alliance with the early Civil Rights Movement. When a few extremists assail the Jewish "misleaders" of the Civil Rights Movement (meaning also those liberals who pioneered the struggle), they are *ipso facto* attacking the traditional Negro leadership. By attacking the Jew (or any white liberal) in the movement, they are attacking "De Lawd" (Dr. Martin Luther King), "Whitey" Young (Whitney Young), and "Uncle Phil" (A. Philip Randolph).

The device is handy, too, because it awakens familiar responses learned from the anti-Semitism of the white world. In a sense, to assail the Jew is almost an acceptable way of attacking the white man without offending the white man. The Negro anti-Semite can be a bad boy with papa's blessing.

In that section of the Negro community that has accepted Muslimism, anti-Semitism finds inspiration and political ties in the Africanism of a Nasser. The Negro is doing here what Nasser would like to do there: conduct a holy war against the Jew.

Finally, Negro anti-Semitism finds secret support in both the extreme right and left wings of American politics. To the white racist, any form of Negro extremism, especially an attack upon liberal Jewry, is ever welcome. First, the extremist acts offer *ex post facto* justification for white racist resistance to Negro rights. Second, conflict between Negro and Jew allows the racist to point up the apparent stupidity and self-destructiveness of all liberalism, including Jewish. Thirdly, the Negro-Jewish conflict tears apart the liberal coalition, the ultimate target of the true reactionary. Counterpointing the strategy of the extreme right is the extreme left, hoping to stir the race war in America as part of a world racist conflict in which the colored people are the revolutionary majority. Left and right together see in the polarization of American politics the inevitable Armageddon, with each extreme certain of its victory.

In response to these developments within the Negro revolution, there are Jews who ask (as well as other white liberals and minorities), "What do they think they are doing?"

The first thing to remember is that there is no "they." There is no Negro "they" anymore than there is a white "we" or a Jewish "We-They." Present tendencies within the Negro community above are merely tendencies: they are not the total Negro community or even most of it. The turn against the Jew is a minority trend within a movement that still is a minority action within the vast Negro community of America. This realization must be held as a constant reminder to balance the inevitable emotional reaction to any act of violence against Jews and to a political ostracism of the Jewish liberal.

If anti-Semitism is an expression of an extremist faction within the Negro movement, then liberal Jewry—together with other liberal elements—should do all it can to strengthen the more sober and responsible leadership in the colored community. This means working with the latter and also creating the social conditions to give credence to their appeals within the Negro community. To do this work, Jewish and liberal leadership must develop sophistication about the Negro and the Negro revolution and not lump all Negroes or even all Negro militants. Only by differentiating between the creative and destructive in the Negro movement can any sector of the white community play a meaningful role in helping this "revolution" become a positive good in the development of the American democracy.

To cite a parallel. For many years, American reactionaries have slowed down our nation's progress by lumping the words "Communist, Socialist, unionist and Jew." It was all "red" to them and they fought it blindly. If their view had prevailed, we would at present be at war with Communist Russia, Socialist England, the AFL-CIO, and Israel. Fortunately, a greater sophistication has enabled policy makers to distinguish not only among all these terms but even between Russian, Yugoslav, and Chinese Communism.

Likewise, liberal (and Jewish) policy toward the Negro and the Negro movement must develop a sophistication that knows the difference between Dr. King, Malcolm X, Stokely Carmichael, Adam Powell, James Farmer and a plain hooligan.

The most difficult assignment in establishing a proper relationship between the Negro and Jewish (also liberal and white) communities falls on the shoulders of Negro leadership. Theirs is a well-nigh impossible task: to arouse a people for a justifiable and militant struggle while checking those primitive passions that express themselves in wanton violence or senseless anti-Semitism. In trying to perform this balancing act, they will be blown about by spontaneous explosions and buffeted by extremist rivals. In their efforts to guide the mass down a traversable road, they will be repeatedly frustrated by obstacles erected in the white world or—even more frustrating— by obstacles left on the road by an accumulated history.

In the anguish of their responsibility, such Negro leaders will be reliving the woes of every revolutionary leader who was as concerned about erecting the new world as destroying the old. Few have succeeded. Normally, those who tear down must die or be pushed aside to make way for a new generation that knows how to build up.

Negro leadership cannot afford this luxury. The Negro is a numerical minority. He is unable to take over the nation and, then, in due time leave it to a second generation to build the new society on the ashes of the old. Minority extremism, exercised by the Negro in America, can never lead to the seizure of power. All it can do is invite the counter-revolution, provide the excuse, occasion and emotional urge for a new slavery.

Our times have been marked by such counter-revolutions in Italy (Mussolini), in Germany (Hitler), in Spain (Franco). America is not immune. And while such counter-revolution in America might well be directed against the Negro, as Hitler's was against the Jew, in the long run, such a return to slavery would bring the dark night of dictatorship to all America—as it did to Italy under Mussolini and Germany under Hitler.

For these reasons, then, the problem of Negro-Jewish relationships goes far beyond the limited question of how these two communities get along with one another when they live in the same or contiguous neighborhoods. In the long run, this is the problem of how a massive and epic revolution in America will ultimately affect the total fabric of the nation—will it lead to the day of liberation or the night of enslavement?

The answer will depend heavily on the sophistication, patience, courage and far-sightedness of leadership in the Negro and in the freedom-loving white community of America, of which the liberal Jews are a part.

HERBERT WEINER

WHEN RABBI Nachman of Bratzlav reminded his followers that "a Jew, with a flick of his finger *here,* can move whole worlds *there,*" he was only reiterating an old Jewish thesis. We have always entertained the notion that Jewish thoughts, Jewish actions and Jewish relationships with other peoples deeply determine the destiny of mankind and the great "happenings" of the lands in which we live. But really, we ought not to impose this notion on the problem of race relationships in America. What Negroes think about Jews as Jews, and what Jews as Jews think about Negroes will be of little consequence for the future of these relationships. Furthermore, what they think will, on the whole, reflect the general mood and stresses of the national Negro-white exchange. This fact seems to be borne out these days by the numerous articles and surveys testing for Negro anti-Semitism and so-called Jewish "backlash." Keeping it in mind may help us to understand how a "dialogue" of the kind envisioned in this symposium may be of value. For who will find it important? The great masses of Negroes and whites whose reactions will determine the course of future events on this issue? The Negro and white leaders whose prime concern is with the reaction of these large groups? I doubt it. Then who will find Negro-Jewish relationships of great concern? My own guess is that it may interest a few Negro leaders who don't want to lose Jewish support and contributions—though most of these have bigger worries to concern them. It may also interest the Jews who want to think through their attitudes toward the Negro revolution from a Jewish point of view—there are not many of these. Actually, the main beneficiaries of the "probe" envisioned in this symposium would be, I would think, the leaders and program planners of those Jewish organizations which have made the Negro problem in America their main focus of interest and energy. Many of these find themselves in the unpleasant psychological predicament of knowing that their leadership is no longer wanted. The activities which a short while ago seemed to be their main *raison d'être* as organizations are now being directed through other channels. And the uncomfortable gap in their personal and organizational lives is made even more painful by an occasional sputtering of anti-Semitism among the very ranks of the people they have been trying to help. That these Jewish leaders and organizations should want to discuss this turn of events is understandable. But they must not exaggerate the effect of their discussions on the development of Negro-white or Negro-Jewish relationships.

On the other hand, such a discussion may have a salutary effect on Jews in their personal thinking and organizational activities. I do not refer now to anti-Semitism—which is surely too inevitable and understandable a phenomenon to make thoughtful Jews alter their attitudes toward the Negro struggle for equality in our land. Why should we expect the Negro to be immune from a virus endemic in the West? Or from the bit of gratification his battered ego can get from identifying with the prejudices of the "whitey" he hates yet wants to emulate? I'm sorry for "Mr. Goldberg" who, doing business in the Negro ghetto, receives a double portion of Negro rage. But in most cases I imagine that "Mr. Goldberg" considers the profit worth the risk and is not entitled to more protection or understanding than would be given any other portion of the white community. I'm sure that Negro leaders recognize the disproportionate amount of help they have received from Jews. But the healthiest part of the Negro revolution is its insistence on seeing help as a right received in partial repayment of a debt, and not as a favor deserving of special thanks. No, the possible salutary effect I see in this kind of discussion has nothing to do with anti-Semitism or with Negro feelings toward Jews. It has to do with Jews and their willingness to think responsibly about the implications for Jewish survival of their preoccupation with integration.

Of course, to question the moral value of integration or to suggest that Judaism is not wholeheartedly committed to its attainment is tantamount to heresy in most Jewish as well as liberal circles. For many of our national Jewish organizations, civil rights and integration (along with Senator Fulbright's attitude toward the Vietnam war) *are* Judaism. And what I have to say on the matter is not new or unknown. Indeed, it is a thought that is usually in the minds of Jewish parents even as they support the heavy concern of their Jewish organizations with Negro problems, and watch with anxious pride the gathering of their children around the banner of "freedom now." To what then am I referring with so much trepidation? I whisper it softly lest I be quickly expelled as a parochial reactionary. But actually the goal of intermingling of groups on every level and in every corner of life—is not a traditional Jewish goal. Surely this needs no textual proof.

The briefest glance at the pattern of Jewish history and the laws of traditional Judaism reveals that separatism, not just between Jews and Negroes, or Negroes and whites, but between all peoples, is far closer to the Jewish dream of an ideal reality than a breaking down of all group barriers. I hasten to shield myself by saying that separatism is not the same as inequality (though I'm not sure). And I realize that integration does not necessarily mean assimilation. But let's leave the level of abstract theory. Can we maintain that it is a sin to perpetuate barriers between people on the basis of accident of birth—ethnic grouping, color, etc.; can we sing the glory of an intermingling which surmounts all "parochial" limitations—yet shake a finger of disapproval at intermarriage? Theoretically, of course, we can. But practically? How many of our young people will grasp the distinction? Is there not some wisdom in the old saying: "If you don't go out in the rain, you don't get wet."

The point is simple, but usually so enraging as to require immediate and fervent reassertion of one's sympathy with the plight of Negroes in our land. Yet to say that a Judaism which regards the struggle for Negro equality as its main or even sole *mitzvah* may be preparing for its own demise, is not to proclaim one's insensitivity to the Negro cause. Nor is it to question either the sincerity or the Judaism of the Rabbis who have made the Negro struggle their main focus of interest. It merely means pointing out the obvious facts that the fight for civil rights can get along without Judaism; that the emotional appeal of a brotherhood that would discard racial, ethnic and religious differences as so many shells of out-dated values, does not bring our young idealists closer to Judaism; that Jewish programming which consists almost exclusively of concern for the Negro can be just as sterile from the point of view of Jewish survival as a Judaism which is interested only in Jews. In short, it is a question of balance—a balance that must result from the fact that not all noble ideals harmonize. The enthusiasm for integration and the yearning of a religious minority for its own survival do at times meet in tragic conflict. In an age when the winds of freedom blow strong and the tree of Judaism has shallow roots and withered blossoms, those who are appointed to guard the life of that tree must consider carefully how and where they will expend their energy.

I realize that this kind of a "balanced" response to what today is surely *the* moral issue in our land, the Negro bid for justice and equality, is less than inspiring. Personally, I find it rather petty, lacking both the vision and poetry of the prophetic seer. It represents the safe and careful limited liberalism of the suburban Jew who is all for integration—in the other community. It understands the Negro thrust to break out of his ghetto, but does not want that thrust to affect in any way the quality of his own child's education. It approves of Fair Housing, but not if it will depreciate one's own property values or push one into a community where he will fear for his family's safety. It understands that we confront a necessary revolution, but it will quickly snatch away the checkbook when faced with the fiery sparks of rage and extremism that are the inevitable concomitants of any genuine revolution. And it has a hurt expression on its face when the object of its sympathy proclaims that it is tired of sympathy. It is indeed a modest idealism. No—I can't say that I find it very inspiring.

I will tell you what I do find inspiring in the way of a Jewish attitude toward revolutionary situations of the kind we face today in America's racial problem. There is a passage written by Abraham Isaac Kuk, the first Chief Rabbi of Palestine (d. 1935), which humbles me. It was not, of course, written with our specific situation in mind. But its message, despite some cabalistic terminology, is clear—for our young "freedom now" demonstrators, for our angry demanders of Black Power, as well as for the frightened upholders of law and order, those that the Rabbi calls, "masters of proportion." I translate it literally, explaining in advance only a few untranslatable Hebrew words. *Tohu* is usually translated as "chaos" but for the mystic, *Tohu* means "pre-form," a world that precedes and is higher than our delimited "world of order." *Hutzpah* is brass, nerve, arrogance—the kind of thing which people say is responsible for the Jewish "backlash." Here is the passage:

"The souls of *Tohu* are higher than the souls of order. (They are very great). They seek much from reality, more than their vessels can endure. They seek very great illumination. Everything which is bounded, delimited, and arranged, they cannot bear. . . .

"They see that they are bound by laws, by limiting conditions which cannot be endlessly expanded . . . so they fall into sadness, despair, anger, and—out of rage—into evil, deliberate sin, degradation, ugliness, abomination, destruction —every kind of evil . . . but the essence of the force which is within them, is the point of holiness. . . .

"Particularly do [these souls] reveal themselves in an end of days' kind of period, a time which precedes the remaking of a world . . . on the eve of redemption *hutzpah* increases. A storm broods, becomes stronger, there is breach after breach, and *hutzpah* escalates. . . .

"These fiery souls show their strength before which no barrier and no limitation can stand, and the weak of the 'formed' world, the masters of 'proportion,' and of 'good manners,' are appalled.—'Who can dwell with consuming fire? Who can dwell with those who would burn up the world!' . . . But the truly powerful will know that this revelation of strength is one of the phenomena which appear for the purpose of perfecting the world, in order to strengthen the power of the people, of the individual, of the world. Only at first this strength appears in the form of *Tohu*, but finally it will be taken from the evil ones and given to the righteous, who with the heroism of lions, through a forceful and clear reason, with strong feeling, in a practical, clear and ordered way, will reveal the true order of construction."

I don't believe that Rabbi Kuk's words need commentary. It is the kind of statement about which the Rabbis say, "and he who understands, will understand."

But it is a statement which has in it a touch of the Messianic vision, and the Messianic vision is a dangerous thing. For if the Lions of Faith who are supposed to show the way to the "true order of construction" do not appear, and the Messianic dream does not materialize, we are liable to fall back into a world which is worse off than the one held together by the petty "masters of proportion." That is why the Jews always countered their Messianic beliefs with the cynical "We'll see that happen when the Messiah comes"—meaning never. And the Rabbis were indeed "masters of proportion," endowed with a strong sense of human limitations.

No, it is not very inspiring, but I think I will take my stand today with those who try to chart a future with this sense of limitation. By a sense of limitation I mean, for example, the understanding (without getting overexcited) that some anti-Semitism in the Negro community is inevitable. A corresponding sense of limitation will help the Negro to understand that Jews will not support causes that condone or overlook such anti-Semitism. By a sense of limitation, I also mean recognition of the fact that skin color has been a source of potential tension and antagonism between peoples all over the world for many thousands of years. That is morally wrong, frustrating, dangerous, etc. But it is a fact which will not quickly be wiped out even by laws enforcing economic and political equality. Some of the Black Power groups are saying this very thing, but what they are saying can be used for constructive as well as destructive purposes.

No, a sense of limitation is not very inspiring, but it can help people reach a kind of modus vivendi and even make some progress toward a better world—while waiting for that dilatory Messiah to arrive.

JACOB J. WEINSTEIN

THERE IS some Negro anti-Semitism and there is some Jewish backlash but the extent of both these phenomena has been exaggerated, as everything seems to be exaggerated in periods of racial tension. Negro anti-Semitism is due to a variety of causes. There is the emotional hold-over of the crucifixion story which semi-literate storefront preachers have told with dramatic fervor. There is the black man's distrust and hostility to the Jew as a member of the white race—the race which shackled him with the chains of slavery and kept him a sec-

ond-class citizen for 103 years after the Emancipation Procla-
mation. It has often happened that the Negro moved into the
Jewish ghetto or next to it and that the Jewish storekeeper,
landlord, installment collector, pawnbroker, dentist, doctor,
lawyer were the only white men with whom he had personal
dealings. The Negro was often not sophisticated enough to
know that impersonal economic factors, the high cost of
doing business in rundown neighborhoods, the general ineq-
uities of our price and fee setting system were the real source
of his problems rather than the specific distributor or professional man. Nor could he understand how the development of
chain-stores and giant corporations with strict quotas on Jews
in the executive suite drove Jews into the marginal small businesses in the slum neighborhoods. The "Goldberg" stereotype
washes out in the wide over-all analysis of economic behavior,
but it does have unfortunate appearances of truth in limited
periods and specific areas. Surely it is the responsibility of
mature Negro leadership to make these larger truths known, but
it is understandable that they may not, under the heavy pressures of their work, give this highest priority. That this same
Negro leadership does not pay sufficient homage to the Jews for
all that the Rosenwalds, the Spingarns, the Jack Greenbergs
and the Kivie Kaplans have done for the amelioration of the
Negro's plight is also understandable. It is a strange perver-
sity of human nature that we often feel ungrateful and even
bitter toward our benefactors when once we regain our feet.
Gratitude is sometimes a form of admission of our former
humiliation.

I base my conviction that Negro anti-Semitism is not of serious proportions on two incidents which occurred in Chicago
in the past several years. The first was the election of Alderman
Len Despres, a Jew, by the voters of the 5th Ward in 1963.
Despres' opponent was a highly respected Negro lawyer,
counsel to Martin Luther King, former officer of the U.S. Army
Air Force. The 5th Ward had a substantial majority of Negro
voters. The campaign was hot and heavy. Blunt appeals were
made for the Negro to capture an important political leverage.
The Democratic City Administration was most unenthusiastic
about Despres, a perennial gadfly to the machine. The Negro
Alderman of the contiguous 4th Ward was unhappy with

Despres as one who set embarrassingly high standards for
Aldermen. But Despres was elected by a comfortable margin
and his heaviest vote was precisely in the Woodlawn district
where the Negro constituency was largest. Not all the heat of
a campaign could persuade the Negro residents of the 5th
Ward to put their racist or religious prejudices above their
respect for a Jew who had served them with zeal, intelligence
and honesty.

The second incident was the murder of two prominent Jewish brothers and a Jewish salesman in an automobile agency by
a disgruntled Negro youth. A misguided Negro Alderman and a
whole platoon of anti-Semitic cranks attempted to blow up
this incident as proof positive of the exploitative greed of
Jewish automobile agency owners. Letters and phone calls to
open end radio programs and to the newspapers were incen-
diary in their raucous ringing on the Shylock theme. But the
attempt proved a dud. The Negro community did not take the
bait. Their legitimate spokesmen did advocate certain reforms
of installment credit practices but kept it on a purely objective basis.

The Muslims have indeed, from time to time, added the white
Jewish devil to the white Christian devil in the list of their
enemies, but it is hard to detect any increase in acts of discrimination. Muslim followers still work for Jewish employers
and still do business with Jewish merchants.

No one has yet made any study in depth or reduced to viable statistical form the strength of the Jewish backlash. It is
obvious that some Jews have been shocked and offended by
Negro vandalism on Jewish stores during the riots in Harlem,
Philadelphia and Watts but the evidence that this destruction
was motivated by anti-Semitism is, so far, negligible. Much
more resentment has been created by Negro Freedom Marchers
in white areas where Jews live. But these Jews have seldom
expressed their resentment openly, nor have they succeeded
in getting a single responsible Jewish agency to deny the
Negro's right to live wherever he can afford to buy or rent
provided only he observed the maintenance and zoning standards of the neighborhood. On the contrary, the Jews of Hyde
Park-Kenwood and the Jews of Rogers Park, Skokie and the
North Shore suburbs have been among the most active work-

ers for Open Occupancy. Jews like Ben Heineman, Eli Aaron and Rabbi Robert Marx were most influential in achieving the Summit Agreement with Dr. Martin Luther King—an agreement by which Dr. King agreed to withhold the march into Cicero on condition that the Chicago city administration and the Real Estate Board would take effective action in opening real estate listings in all parts of the city to prospective Negro tenants.

Perhaps the most compelling evidence that the Jewish backlash is only the occasional mumbling of some Jews who approved the ultimate ideal of integration but became queasy when they faced the facts—the here and now of it—lies in the fact that there has been hardly a peep from the many young Jewish college graduates who have been blocked or detoured from the executive suite because it is good politics and good economics for corporations to have visible dark faces in management echelons. In the Post Office, where rapid upgrading of Negroes has sometimes been at the expense of Jews in the department, there have been very few complaints.

The backlash takes annoying but not hurtful forms such as reminding the Negro that we Jews had it much worse in the ghetto and that we raised ourselves up by our own bootstraps, that we learned to convert our disabilities into the spur of harder work and greater achievement. If the Negro does become anti-Semitic it will in no small measure be due to our throwing this patronizing homily at him disregarding the fact that the slave trader made certain that the African Negro would be separated from his cultural roots and his native religious supports.

In any discussion of the Negro problem, it is well to be reminded that the most meaningful benefits that come to the Negro are those which are a by-product of general improvements in the body politic rather than those which come about as a shift in the allocation of power. We recall that the greatest single benefit that came to the Jews—especially the working class Jews—was a consequence of the rise of trade unionism, that the greatest breakthrough in higher education came when the nation, through public and private funds, made teachers and colleges available to a larger part of our population rather than through liberalization of quotas. So, too, will it be with the Negro when better education, better housing, better job opportunities are available because of advances in the general democratic processes, in the further liberalization of our economy, in a more effective implementation of our philosophy of religious and cultural pluralism. When we ask the Jew to beware of the "Black Power" advocates and the Black Muslim separatists we ask of him the most tantalizing discretion, since he must reject any analogies between Negro Nationalism and Jewish Zionist Nationalism, as well as any attempt to equate the Negro migration with the migration of other immigrant groups. These are fascinating analogies but they lead to dead ends.

Nor will it be simple to advocate the priority of struggle for the general improvement of civic, economic and educational opportunities and at the same time to accept the validity of compensatory preference as a starting concession. But life is seldom nobly consistent and our own long, tortuous trek through history should help us understand that the way to make the crooked straight often is a serpentine way.

NOTES ON CONTRIBUTORS

JOEL CARMICHAEL is the author of *The Death of Jesus, A Short History of the Russian Revolution,* and *The Shaping of the Arabs.*

ARTHUR A. COHEN is the author of *The Natural and the Supernatural Jew,* and of numerous articles dealing with Jewish and Christian theology. His first novel, *The Carpenter Years,* was published in January by New American Library.

JACOB COHEN taught history for seven years at Yale and Brandeis, and for a year edited a magazine for CORE.

LUCY S. DAWIDOWICZ is a researcher at the American Jewish Committee and author of numerous articles in *Commentary* and other journals.

HOWARD FAST is the author of such well-known books as *Citizen Tom Paine* and *Spartacus.*

MYRON M. FENSTER is Rabbi of the Shelter Rock Jewish Center, Roslyn, New York.

LESLIE A. FIEDLER'S most recent book is *The Last Jew in America.*

ROLAND B. GITTELSOHN is Rabbi of Temple Israel, Boston, Massachusetts.

JACOB GLATSTEIN is the well-known Yiddish poet, novelist, and critic.

B. Z. GOLDBERG, the noted Yiddish and English author and journalist, is a columnist for the Yiddish-language daily *Day-Morning Journal.*

HARRY GOLDEN, editor of *The Carolina Israelite,* is the well-known author of *Only in America, For 2¢ Plain, A Little Girl is Dead,* and numerous other popular books.

BEN HALPERN, author of *The Idea of the Jewish State* and

The American Jew, is a member of the faculty of Brandeis University.

ARTHUR HERTZBERG, Rabbi of Temple Emanu-el in Englewood, New Jersey, and author of *The Zionist Idea,* is Lecturer in History on the graduate faculty of Columbia University and visiting Associate Professor of History at Rutgers University.

PAUL JACOBS is author of the recently published *Is Curly Jewish?* His new book on the failures of an American city, Los Angeles, was published last spring.

HORACE M. KALLEN, Research Professor in Social Philosophy at the New School for Social Research, and Distinguished Seminar Professor at Long Island University, is author of numerous books in the fields of social psychology and philosophy, among them *The Liberal Spirit, Patterns of Progress, Cultural Pluralism and the American Idea,* and *Of Them Which Say They Are Jews.*

C. ERIC LINCOLN, Professor of Sociology at Portland State College, is author of *The Black Muslims in America* and *My Face Is Black.*

WILL MASLOW is Executive Director of the American Jewish Congress.

FLOYD B. MCKISSICK is National Director of CORE.

ARYEH NEIER is Executive Director of the New York Civil Liberties Union.

MAURICE SAMUEL, the well-known writer and lecturer, is author of the recently published *Blood Accusation: The Strange History of the Beiliss Case.*

STEVEN S. SCHWARZSCHILD, editor of *Judaism,* is a Rabbi and a member of the Department of Philosophy at Washington University, St. Louis, Missouri.

BEN B. SELIGMAN is Professor of Economics and Director of the Labor Relations and Research Center at the University of Massachusetts.

WILLIAM STRINGFELLOW is author of *My People is the Enemy* and the recently published *Dissenter in a Great Society.*

MARIE SYRKIN, editor of the *Jewish Frontier,* is author of a study of the New York Public School system, *Your School, Your Children*.

GUS TYLER, Assistant President of the ILGWU, is author of *The Labor Revolution; Trade Unionism in a New America*.

HERBERT WEINER, author of *The Wild Goats of Ein Gedi*, is Rabbi of Temple Israel, South Orange, New Jersey.

JACOB J. WEINSTEIN is Rabbi of K.A.M. Temple in Chicago.